"Paul Harvey was a true pioneer and the greatest ambassador—and perhaps performer—in the history of radio."

RUSH LIMBAUGH
Nationally syndicated radio host and political commentator

"Paul Harvey was not one of the great American broadcasters; he was the gold standard of American broadcasters. He has no equals or peers—he stands alone as a classic icon. His patriotism, faith, and bedrock values were a source of stability and consistency in an otherwise unstable and chaotic time. His golden voice reassured us, entertained us, encouraged us, and challenged us. If God were to assume a human voice, I believe it would sound a lot like Paul Harvey's."

MIKE HUCKABEE
Former Arkansas governor and current host of Huckabee *on Fox News and his radio commentary* The Huckabee Report

"I'm like practically every broadcaster in America: an entire career spent emulating, respecting, and admiring the iconic Paul Harvey. Radio—and the country—have been enriched by the wit, wisdom, patriotism, charm, and impact of this most amazing man."

MIKE GALLAGHER
Radio host of The Mike Gallagher Show

"The life of Paul Harvey was one of unfailing graciousness. He was the very model of an old-school gentleman, quick with a compliment or inquiry about one's family or work. Paul endeared himself to me with what I believe was a sincere reaction to people: he was always grateful, yet somewhat puzzled, that there were so many who were anxious to meet him."

JIM BOHANNON
Host of The Jim Bohannon Show

A TRIBUTE

STEPHEN MANSFIELD & DAVID A. HOLLAND

PAUL HARVEY'S
America

THE LIFE, ART, AND FAITH OF A MAN WHO TRANSFORMED RADIO AND INSPIRED A NATION

Visit Tyndale's exciting Web site at www.tyndale.com

TYNDALE and Tyndale's quill logo are registered trademarks of Tyndale House Publishers, Inc.

Paul Harvey's America: The Life, Art, and Faith of a Man Who Transformed Radio and Inspired a Nation

Designed by Dan Farrell

Published in association with the literary agency of Esther Fedorkevich, Fedd and Company Inc., 9759 Concord Pass, Brentwood, TN 37027.

Scripture quotations are taken from *The Holy Bible*, King James Version.

Library of Congress Cataloging-in-Publication Data

Mansfield, Stephen, date.
   Paul Harvey's America : the life, art, and faith of a man who transformed radio and inspired a nation / by Stephen Mansfield and David A. Holland.
     p. cm.
   Includes bibliographical references.
   ISBN 978-1-4143-3450-9 (hc)
    1. Harvey, Paul, 1918-2009.   2. Radio broadcasters—United States—Biography.
I. Holland, David A. II. Title.
PN1991.4.H34M36 2009
791.4402'8092—dc22
[B]   2009017624

Printed in the United States of America

15   14   13   12   11   10   09
7   6   5   4   3   2   1

To our fathers,
LEE MANSFIELD *&* JOHN HOLLAND

CONTENTS

ACKNOWLEDGMENTS

I discovered in the 1970s that love for radio that an older generation of Americans had long before found. I lived in Berlin, Germany, in those years, the son of an army officer during the Cold War. Satellite TV had yet to evolve into what we know now, so while my friends back home in the States were basking in the joys of cable TV, I was often to be found pressed against a radio to hear Casey Kasem count down the hits on Armed Forces Radio. This is when I discovered Paul Harvey. His voice became America for me, as fun as old men telling jokes on a small-town square and filled with the wisdom of ages gone by. And he did something I thought no one could do: he made me love the past. His *The Rest of the Story* helped me see beyond the numbing dates and dead people of history class to the dramatic nobility of generations before. In time, history became my passion too, and I live in the knowledge that it was Paul Harvey who first stirred this love. How very grateful I am.

David Holland has been a valiant partner in this project. His wisdom and gentle strength have been gifts to us all while we worked, and they remind me that he has earned the nickname "Yoda" for good reason. Beverly Darnall Mansfield is my partner in life as well as in literature, and her wisdom graces both these pages and my days. And Esther Fedorkevich, agent and friend, has tended our partnership with Tyndale House Publishers, assuring that this book would be as much a delight to write as we hope it will be to read. My gratitude to each of these.

Stephen Mansfield

I am profoundly grateful to Stephen Mansfield for extending the opportunity to join him in telling the story of this extraordinary American. My thanks also goes to Beverly Darnall Mansfield for her support and her sensitivity to making this story accessible to the widest possible audience. Also to Jon Simpson for holding down the fort back at the offices of Cobalt Bridge Multichannel. And to my bride, Tracy, for her amazing encouragement and support.

David A. Holland

Both of us, Stephen and David, wish to express our deepest gratitude to Chartwell Literary Group (http://www.chartwellliterary.com). Their skill and professionalism have made this book a joy to write.

FOREWORD

IF YOUR EXPERIENCE IN LIFE has been anything like mine, you probably remember driving in your car or sitting in your home and hearing these words come over your radio: "Hello, Americans. This is Paul Harvey. Stand by for news!" Like me, you very likely leaned in, turned up the volume, and got ready for the trademark Paul Harvey experience.

What would follow was always entertaining. Paul's signature voice would carry you on a tour of that day's America, a tour that ranged from the critical newspaper headlines to Aunt Sissy's candy shop in Topeka, from the doings of presidents to the funny thing that happened to Farmer Jensen when he went to his barn early one morning. This was what made Paul Harvey one of the great broadcasters of our time: his ability to bring both the grand and the commonplace of American life to his listeners.

Yet Paul did more than simply report on America. He also loved America, and he made certain we knew this in every broadcast, every voice inflection, and every lesson that he taught us through all those years.

Paul Harvey understood that America is unique in human history, a nation founded in a vision of freedom that was new in the world at the time. He was right when he located the greatness of America in the character of her people, in their industry, and in the goodness of their hopes. He knew that it was sacrifice and hard work that had made America strong. And he knew something else too. He knew what Alexis de Tocqueville had come to understand: that if you search for the meaning of America, you must look not so much in her halls of government as in the pews of her churches.

Paul Harvey wanted us never to forget what it cost our forefathers to give us this great nation. And so in every broadcast, particularly in his famous *The Rest of the Story* series, he taught us what we often did not know of our valiant Founding Fathers and of the stalwart souls who have gone before us. He gave us broad shoulders to stand upon if we were willing, and he showed us the patriot's way.

This was the way Paul Harvey had chosen. It was why he spoke out against communist usurpers in the 1950s, against the excesses of the 1960s, and against the hedonism of the 1970s and 1980s. It was also why he even got himself arrested for climbing the fence of a secret test facility to demonstrate that security there was not what it was supposed to be. He was willing to put his feet where his words were, whatever the opposition, whatever the price.

Now that he is no longer with us, there are likely to be many biographies of this great and beloved man. But what we need in our troubled times is something more: we need to rekindle our own version of his love for America, to awaken our own passion to protect her at any cost. This is what Stephen Mansfield and David Holland have given us a chance to do. They have told us of Paul Harvey the man, but they have also told of Paul Harvey's vision for America. This is a vision we desperately need to renew today.

So pull aside and take some time to read this vitally important book. Our times are in crisis, and we need a people to arise who love their country more than life and who are willing to help rebuild the Founders' vision wherever it is threatened. This is what *Paul Harvey's America* can help you do, and believe me, there has never been a greater need.

Sean Hannity

INTRODUCTION

HIGH ABOVE BUSTLING MICHIGAN AVENUE—Chicago's "Magnificent Mile"—on a crisp autumn day, a well-appointed conference room is buzzing. A handful of power-suited executives, lawyers, and administrative assistants are milling about, awaiting the arrival of the couple who are the focus of the day's important business.

There is a contract to be signed, a contract that is the result of one of the fiercest and most remarkable bidding wars in the history of the news and entertainment industry.

As is often the case in the media business, this is a youngish crowd. There is scarcely a gray hair to be found, as the average age in the room is struggling to rise north of forty. Helping to pull that average upward just a little is Traug Keller—the middle-aged president of ABC Radio Networks. He heads the victorious company in the competition to sign this media star and his business-partner wife.

The female half of the power couple—the business and strategic brain behind her husband's rise to world fame—once said, "We live our lives by the second hand of the clock." So it surprises no one that at the exact moment the meeting is scheduled to begin, an impeccably dressed man and woman more than twice the room's average age sweep through the mahogany doorway all smiles and energy and poise and grace. The chatter in the room hushes as all eyes turn to the pair standing hand in hand at the head of the long conference table. Then formality gives way to laughter, handshakes, and hugs all around.

It is November 1, 2000. Paul Harvey and his cherished wife of sixty years, "Angel"—ages eighty-two and eighty-four, respectively—are there to sign a new contract with the radio network that has been their professional home for the previous five decades. It is a deal that will pay them more than $100 million over the next ten years.

You read that right.

One of America's leading broadcast radio networks gave an octogenarian a ten-year commitment at a rate of $10 million each year. And did so happily.

In the face of these facts, you might well ask, "Who *is* this man?"

You see, it was not sentimentality or charity that drove this decision. Oh, to be sure, there was an enormous reservoir of affection at the company for the national icon who had made his professional home behind ABC microphones since the mid-1940s and whose broadcasting career had touched each of seven decades. But it was clear-eyed, calculated business logic that moved ABC Radio Networks to tender an offer that Traug Keller described, with only slight hyperbole, as "the biggest deal ever cut with a radio personality"[1] and to extend it to the man he called "one of the most influential Americans of our time."[2]

This was the same calculus that moved three other competing networks to aggressively pursue Paul Harvey—a man who was born two years before the first commercial radio broadcast ever aired.

Paul Harvey was a coveted property at eighty-two because he was still—by every measure—the most-listened-to voice in America. And industry insiders estimated advertising revenues built around the twin franchises of *Paul Harvey News and Comment* and *The Rest of the Story* to be more than $40 million annually.

It was widely known that advertisers were lined up to pay a premium for the opportunity to sponsor just one of the daily Paul Harvey radio programs. But getting a place at that coveted table required much more than simply showing up with a fat checkbook. If the man the *Chicago Tribune* called "the greatest salesman in the history of radio"[3] was going to pitch your product, it, and you, had to pass muster. He never took on an advertiser until he had tried the product, found it excellent and beneficial, and had met the leadership behind the company that made it.

Adding to the allure of sponsoring Paul Harvey was the sheer scarcity of opportunity. There are only so many commercial slots in a short newscast. And those advertisers who got on board tended to stay a long time because of the product-moving power of Paul Harvey's endorsement.

Bankers Life and Casualty was an advertiser for over thirty years. Neutrogena was a delighted sponsor for twenty years. "And I think they would both still be with us if the companies hadn't been sold," Harvey once lamented. Utilizing the play with words that was one of his hallmarks, he once told a reporter, "I am fiercely loyal to those willing to put their money where my mouth is."

And they were loyal in return.

Thus, it was no surprise that other networks made every effort to lure Paul and Angel Harvey away from ABC as their contract expiration coincided with the expiration of the millennium.

Naturally, Angel, as Paul's longtime producer and guardian of his professional interests, got a kick out of the fact that, in spite of living in a youth-obsessed media culture, they were still being pursued. In a day in which Hollywood writers were reckoned over the hill and put out to pasture at thirty-five, she and her husband were hot commodities in their eighties! She would later confide to one reporter, "It was fun. These other radio companies were coming to us and offering us so much. One man asked what kind of jet plane Paul liked, and said, 'How would he like a Gulfstream?'"[4]

Paul, too, was gratified that these other companies thought enough of his vigor and vitality to place a big, multiyear wager on him.

But in the end, it was not perks, prestige, or pay that drove the couple's decision. It was the intense premium they had always placed on loyalty. So, after much prayer—"We both strongly believe in praying for guidance," Paul told a reporter at the time—they let ABC Radio know they planned to re-up with the network that had delivered Paul Harvey's unmistakable voice to Americans through five decades of war, recession, crisis, technological transformation, and cultural upheaval.

Of course, saying yes to ABC meant saying no to the other offers. Ever the gentleman—unfailingly humble, gracious, and grateful—Paul Harvey quickly followed that decision with hand-typed letters to each of the other major suitors. He thanked them for their interest and explained the reasons for the choice he and Angel had made together. One of the other network heads wrote back, promising, "We'll reopen talks in 10 years. I'll get you yet."[5]

Of that compliment, a smiling Angel Harvey wryly noted, "That shows a wonderful faith in our constitution."

You already know what Paul Harvey would have called "the rest of the story." That second opportunity to bid for Paul Harvey's services will not come. It cannot. Angel Harvey passed away in 2008 after sixty-eight years of marriage to her beloved Paul. And as is so often the case with souls tightly braided together by strands of affection, devotion, trials, and time, Paul followed her a mere ten months later. He had, it seems, forgotten how to live without her.

His death on that last day of February 2009 put the punctuation mark on the final chapter of a most fascinating story. He died at a time much like that at which he had been born—with his nation wearily, reluctantly, at war. In between those opening and closing pages hides not just a chronicle of an extraordinary man's extraordinary life but something more.

We took him for granted, of course. It was easy to assume that Paul Harvey would always be on our radios. After all, he had been a comforting fixture there as long as almost any living American could remember.

Tens of millions were intimately acquainted with the voice, as if it belonged to a close family member. For almost any person over the age of thirty, the words "Hello, Americans" were all they needed. Like several generations before them, they came to expect that whatever words followed that cheery greeting would be interesting, authentic, and delivered with a captivating, almost musical artistry.

Yes, many knew the voice. But surprisingly few know much about the remarkable life of the man to whom it belonged. After his passing, a *Chicago Tribune* columnist who knew him well remarked that Harvey's "career—his whole life, really—was packed with the sort of surprises, superlatives, bold statements and seemingly small details that, woven together, also made up a great Paul Harvey broadcast."[6]

Born in 1918, the year World War I ended, Harvey lived through the birth of broadcasting and the Great Depression. His calling and influence made him both witness to, and often a key participant in, the historic dramas of World War II, the Cold War, the convulsive cultural turmoil of the sixties, the national malaise of the seventies, the renewal of the eighties, and militant Islam's slow-motion declaration of war on the West in the nineties, which culminated in the worst attack on American soil since Pearl Harbor.

Yes, Paul Harvey helped us think clearly and with needed perspective about most of the colossal events of the twentieth century. But isn't it interesting that he is just as fondly remembered for speaking to us about everyday people and their mundane, middle-American milestones? A mention of a peace treaty on the other side of the world was often followed by a small-town item, like one from Cassville, in which we learned that farmer White has "a Watusi cow with the largest horns anybody has ever seen." A quick mention of the latest high-profile Hollywood divorce would invariably be dwarfed by a glowing tribute to a Wisconsin dairy-farming couple celebrating their sixtieth wedding anniversary.

Indeed, it is unfortunate, tragic even, that a storyteller as gifted as Paul Harvey never found the time to tell us his own tale in vivid detail. No autobiography of Paul Harvey ever emerged from his beloved IBM Selectric typewriter. Perhaps his only son, Paul Jr., a gifted writer in his own right, will do the world that service one day soon. After all "Young Paul," as his parents referred to him all his life, was the principal writer of *The Rest of the Story* feature for its entire thirty-two-year run.

It is clear that the life of Paul Harvey merits a full and thorough biography. That, however, is not the aim of this book. Here you will certainly discover a great deal about the key events in Paul Harvey's intriguing journey. But what interests us is not only his life but also his *times*. And more important, what his words and values as projected through those times can tell us about the America he loved so passionately and championed so unapologetically.

Yes, it is fitting that the life of the twentieth century's greatest American storyteller itself makes for a truly great American story. Yet as that story unfolds, you are likely to find that there is more than inspiration and perspective in the telling. There is truth. Forgotten, neglected, even rejected, truth.

There are some who suspect that something in America died with Paul Harvey—or is dying as time relentlessly claims the remnants of what has come to be known as "the greatest generation." Something precious and noble and good. And though Paul Harvey is gone and his generation is now passing away, perhaps the flame of that American spirit can be rekindled in remembering who they were and what they meant to us. Paul Harvey, ever the optimist, would have believed so.

On the pages that follow, then, let's gather round the fire of this amazing life and warm ourselves in its good-humored glow. Perhaps we'll take away a few sparks and embers that can light our way in the gathering gloom of the twenty-first century.

CHAPTER 1

A STUBBORN REVERENCE

*"A policeman? . . . Of all men, he is at once
the most needed and most unwanted."*

PAUL HARVEY

A LITTLE BOY PLAYS IN HIS PAJAMAS on the floor by the freshly trimmed Christmas tree. His big sister, twelve, reads a book by the fire. Their mother, Anna Aurandt, is in the kitchen baking the first of what will be several waves of holiday pastries and pies that reflect her Danish heritage.

The Christmas of 1921 is only a week away, and life is pretty good. The "war to end all wars" is a fading memory. President Warren G. Harding, who had campaigned on the slogan "A Return to Normalcy," has seemingly delivered on that promise. Mr. Marconi's amazing invention is finally finding widespread application as the first commercial radio stations (and affordable radios) are popping up all over the countryside. Indeed, the twenties have already begun to roar.

Little Paul Harvey Aurandt would ordinarily be in bed well before this nine o'clock hour, but he has received a special dispensation to wait up for his father, who is expected at any moment.

Harry Aurandt is a police officer in the thriving oil boomtown of Tulsa, Oklahoma. At the age of forty-eight, he has risen through the ranks to become the assistant to Tulsa's police commissioner. On this night, Harry and a fellow off-duty officer have slipped out to do a little rabbit hunting in the woods just beyond the east edge of town. When little Paul saw his father put on his heavy coat and swing the small-bore shotgun over his shoulder after dinner, he begged to come along but was given a firm "No, Son."

"But I won't be out too late," his father said. "You can wait up, and I'll show you what we got if we do any good."

Half past nine comes and goes, and a disappointed but sleepy little man is sent off to bed. When her husband doesn't return by 10:30, the boy's mother starts to worry in earnest. Then comes the urgent knock at the door and a winded uniformed officer on her porch.

"It's Harry, ma'am. He's been shot. Some robbers . . . he's at the hospital . . . it's pretty bad."

A neighbor is roused to stay with the children as Anna accompanies the officer to the hospital with a siren slicing through the still winter night. Her husband is alive and conscious when she arrives, but he is suffering badly from gunshot wounds to the chest, abdomen, and leg.

According to the ensuing investigation, Harry Aurandt and police detective Ike Wilkinson had been leaving the hunting area in their vehicle when they came across a stalled car on the rural road.[1] Stopping to render assistance to a motorist they assumed was lost or having car trouble, they rolled down the windows and called out. In response, they encountered four handguns pointed at them through the curtained windows of a Buick touring sedan, along with a profanity-laced demand for their wallets. The moment the bandits spotted the officer's shotguns, however, they opened fire. In the hail of .38 caliber lead, Detective Wilkinson was hit in both legs. He would survive, but he had walked his last field in search of game.

Two of the bullets that hit Officer Aurandt were later found to have punctured his lung and liver. Nevertheless, Harry was able to drive both of them about a mile to the nearest farmhouse for help.

Two days later Harry Harrison Aurandt succumbed to his injuries with Anna at his side.

The little boy who would grow up to give America a fatherly voice had lost his father. He did so without ever having the opportunity to get to know him, much less tag along with him on a rabbit hunt. In fact, Paul Harvey was left without a solitary clear, treasured memory of his dad.

What he got as consolation was a hero.

Fast-forward more than seventy years from that Christmas of heart-ache, and we find Paul Harvey standing before a large banquet hall filled with police officers and their families. He is addressing a meeting of the National Law Enforcement Officers Memorial Fund, a group dedicated to encouraging support for police personnel as well as maintaining a museum and memorial to fallen officers in our nation's capital.

It is this group's annual candlelight vigil, the somber culmination of Police Week 1992. Among Harvey's words to the solemn assembly this night are these:

> [It was] noted that my father was a lawman in the early dirt street days of Tulsa, Oklahoma. He was shot to death when I was three. So surely at least some of my stubborn reverence for a policeman's uniform dates back to that night before Christmas, many lonely years ago.
>
> In five decades on the news beat I have seen men defile that uniform and disgrace it; I have seen more than one fat hand on the end of the long arm of the law; but I have seen thousands wear that uniform with dignity and decency and pride.
>
> A policeman is a composite of what all of us are: A mingling of saint, sinner . . . dust and deity.
>
> A multiplicity of competing media x-rays any instance of

dishonesty or brutality because that is what news *is*: Something *in*congruous, *ex*ceptional, *un*usual.

If you forget everything else Paul Harvey had to say tonight, please remember this: Less than one-half of one percent of policemen and/or policewomen misfit that uniform. I said less than one-half of one percent of law officers misfit that uniform, and that is a better average than you will find among clergymen.[2]

His presence at that event was no random booking of a generic celebrity speaker. By 1992 Paul Harvey had long established himself as one of the most powerful media friends that police officers had. Indeed, one of the hallmarks of Paul Harvey's life and work was the use of his platform to encourage support for law enforcement, especially the street cop. As a result, countless police organizations across the land considered him a friend.

He earned much of that reputation for what he termed a "stubborn reverence for the policeman's uniform" in those convulsive years in the 1960s and 1970s when a culture of protest, covered by an increasingly sympathetic news establishment, put police departments on the defensive across the country.

By the midsixties, America's decaying inner cities and college campuses were simmering pressure cookers of anger, frustration, and revolutionary zeal. In the cities, the civil rights movement had split into two adversarial camps over methods and values. One camp, headed by Dr. Martin Luther King Jr., was committed to pursuing a strategy of nonviolent resistance and high-profile awareness raising. The other, poisoned by a toxic infusion of Marxist ideology and radical Islamic theology, manifested itself in organizations like the Black Panthers.

Police efforts to keep order and enforce local laws often made them flash points of controversy in a volatile tinderbox. In 1965 it was a simple traffic stop for suspected drunken driving that somehow escalated into the Watts race riots in South-Central Los Angeles.

As the great unraveling of the 1960s progressed, a Left-leaning news media became increasingly prone to publicize claims of "police brutality" and cast law enforcement in a negative light. Paul Harvey, on the other hand, saw the vast majority of police officers in a no-win situation, valiantly doing their best under extremely difficult circumstances.

He spoke for tens of thousands of demoralized law enforcement officers and for much of Middle America when in 1970 he wrote a newspaper column that ended up tacked to the bulletin boards of police stations across the nation:

> What is a policeman made of? He, of all men, is once the most needed and the most unwanted. He's a strangely nameless creature who is "sir" to his face and "fuzz" to his back. He must be such a diplomat that he can settle differences between individuals so that each will think he won.
>
> But . . . if the policeman is neat, he's conceited; if he's careless, he's a bum. If he's pleasant, he's flirting; if not, he's a grouch. He must make an instant decision which would require months for a lawyer to make.
>
> But . . . if he hurries, he's careless; if he's deliberate, he's lazy. He must be first to an accident and infallible with his diagnosis. He must be able to start breathing, stop bleeding, tie splints and, above all, be sure the victim goes home without a limp. Or expect to be sued.
>
> The police officer must know every gun, draw on the run, and hit where it doesn't hurt. He must be able to whip two men twice his size and half his age without damaging his uniform and without being "brutal."
>
> If you hit him, he's a coward. If he hits you, he's a bully.
>
> A policeman must know everything—and not tell. He must know where all the sin is and not partake. A policeman must, from a single strand of hair, be able to describe the crime, the

weapon and the criminal—and tell you where the criminal is hiding. But . . . if he catches the criminal, he's lucky; if he doesn't, he's a dunce.

If he gets promoted, he has political pull; if he doesn't, he's a dullard. The policeman must chase a bum lead to a dead-end, stake out ten nights to tag one witness who saw it happen—but refused to remember.

The policeman must be a minister, a social worker, a diplomat, a tough guy and a gentleman.

And, of course, he'd have to be genius . . . for he will have to feed a family on a policeman's salary.[3]

It is no accident that when Paul Harvey passed away, some of the strongest and most heartfelt expressions of appreciation and loss came from the law enforcement community. Street cops knew they'd lost their most articulate and influential friend. He was not a knee-jerk apologist but a clear-eyed, understanding ally.

And those race riots that set large swaths of Los Angeles aflame in 1965?

Forty-four years earlier, policemen in a little Oklahoma boom-town were struggling to contain that incident's inverse corollary—rampaging whites burning down black-owned businesses and killing all those who got in their way.

Yes, seven months before he fell victim to an outlaw's bullet, Harry Aurandt was among those Tulsa police officers trying to rein in what became "the costliest incident of racial violence in America's history."[4]

• • •

The Tulsa, Oklahoma, that welcomed the birth of Paul Harvey Aurandt on September 4, 1918, was a complicated and contradictory place.

The city sat at the intersection of America's Midwest, Southwest, and Deep South, and displayed characteristics of all three regions—an exotic hybrid blending of Kansas City, Dallas, and Montgomery on a raw, more concentrated scale.

In 1900, Tulsa had been little more than a smattering of wooden and brick buildings on the north bank of the Arkansas River. Oklahoma was seven years away from even becoming a state. Then in 1901, wildcatters discovered oil just across the river at Red Fork. Four years later, nearby Glenpool became the site of the largest oil strike the nation had yet seen, and the boom was on.

As oil overwhelmed cattle as the primary driver of the thriving economy, great fortunes were being amassed by local oilmen with names like William Skelly, Waite Phillips, Harry S. Sinclair, Erle P. Halliburton, and Jean Paul Getty, and those fortunes in turn financed a robust arts and culture scene in Tulsa.

By 1918, the city's population had swelled to nearly seventy thousand. But amid the shiny, new multistory buildings, Greek revival mansions, and breathtaking technological advances of the time walked the ghosts of the Civil War. Some of those ghosts were living, breathing men.

In most American cities in 1918, Fourth of July parades invariably featured elderly Civil War veterans in fraying old uniforms of either blue or gray, many with artificial legs or missing arms. This was the case in Tulsa as well except that one was likely to see both blue *and* gray colors in the parade. The bitter and bloody, slavery-centered rivalry between nearby Kansas and Missouri had spilled across the border as soon as the Tulsa area opened up for settlement.

Here, former Union loyalists from Kansas lived next door to ex-slaveholders from Arkansas. Meanwhile, elderly emancipated slaves and their sons and daughters lived a separated existence "across the tracks."

In fact, Tulsa had one of the most vibrant and successful black communities in the nation. Though segregated from most of white Tulsa by both force of law and cultural habit, the black Greenwood district of Tulsa thrived commercially, culturally, and spiritually. The area that had already achieved a national reputation as the "Negro Wall Street" seemed to be a living, working validation of the self-reliance philosophy of Booker T. Washington. Greenwood's autonomous success even tempted some to believe that the "separate but equal" approach to dealing with the issue of race and public education—the one the U.S. Supreme Court put forth in its controversial *Plessy v. Ferguson* decision of 1896—might actually work.

All of that progress and promise was obliterated on May 31, 1921, when escalating rumors that a white girl had been assaulted in a department store elevator by a black youth set segments of the city on edge. It ultimately led to a rampage that left thirty-five blocks of the Greenwood district in ashes and more than three hundred citizens— the vast majority of them black—dead.

Sadly, the Tulsa of Paul Harvey's childhood was home to men who perpetrated one of the most horrific crimes of racist mob violence in our nation's history. But it was also a city that contained a significant segment of white citizens who were truly horrified by the hatred and violence. They were profoundly shamed that their neighbors and coworkers could be capable of such cruelty, and they did what they could to protect, assist, and restore the victims.

Prominent among the latter were the leaders and members of the Aurandts' family church, First Presbyterian. In fact, on the night of the riots, as an angry lynch mob of thugs gathered at the courthouse demanding that the accused young black man, Dick Rowland, be handed over to them, the Aurandts' minister ran to the scene and bravely confronted the armed crowd, pleading with them to go home and let the legal system do its job.[5]

That pastor, Dr. Charles W. Kerr, had come to the Indian Territory in 1898 as a Scots Presbyterian missionary to the tribes. He had taken the helm of First Presbyterian in 1900. Seven years later he cofounded the University of Tulsa. But on that night in 1918, he assumed the mantle of fiery Reformer John Knox and tried to face down a seething, hate-filled mob. He did not prevail, but the courage and conscience Kerr displayed on that awful night are remembered in Scotland to this day.[6]

• • •

It is impossible to know for sure, but Harry and Anna Aurandt must surely have found Tulsa's racially charged undercurrents and persistent antebellum baggage bewildering.

Anna Dagmar Christensen was born in Denmark in 1883 and immigrated with her parents to the United States when she was very young. Her family eventually settled in the St. Louis, Missouri, area.

Harry Harrison Aurandt hailed from an area of central Pennsylvania that had received many waves of German immigrants over the first hundred years of European settlement. Harry was born in Martinsburg, Pennsylvania, in 1873 and was most likely the descendant of Germans who came to the American colonies fleeing religious persecution in the early eighteenth century. To this day, far more people with the German surname Aurandt (or the alternate spelling, Aurand) live in Pennsylvania than in any other state.

Most biographical sketches of Paul Harvey note that he claimed to be the product of "five generations of Baptist preachers." This may be accurate, but it's also a little misleading. When most modern Americans hear the descriptor "Baptist," they think of Billy Graham or Jerry Falwell.

In fact, most of those Germans making the hazardous crossing to the New World between 1719 and 1729 were German Baptists or "Dunkards," an Anabaptist offshoot of the German Reformed movement. It is out of this tradition that Harry Aurandt surely sprang.

Other nearby branches on this complex family tree of sects include the Brethren, the Amish, and the Mennonites, groups as well-known for their pacifism as their piety.

Regarding his spiritual heritage, Paul Harvey once wondered out loud if he had perhaps inherited "an overdose of righteousness." He never admitted to personally feeling a pull toward the ministry, though. "The pulpit is a responsibility infinitely higher than any I aspire to," he once told an interviewer.

Nevertheless, he brought a circuit-riding preacher's zeal to his calling, along with an evangelist's flair for painting word pictures. A strong sense of morality also characterized his commentaries right up to his last day on the air. Rejecting the moral relativism that permeates most news coverage in our time, he said, "I can't separate goodness and badness from any day's news and make sense of it."[7]

At some point Harry Aurandt made his way to Missouri, where he met and married his Danish bride. And they, in turn, headed for the freshly minted state of Oklahoma to begin their lives together.

How wild and foreign a place Tulsa must have seemed to them both, and yet the record indicates they wasted no time in putting down roots and establishing themselves in the community. A search of the newspaper archives of that period reveals numerous mentions of Anna Aurandt in the society columns—participating in luncheons, teas, and high-profile church events. Meanwhile, her husband rose to become the right hand of the police commissioner, a role we would call administrative assistant today.

They shared a modest but tastefully appointed two-story home on East Fifth Place, a middle-class street of turn-of-the-century bungalows lying immediately east of downtown Tulsa. The house stands to this day.

When Paul Harvey passed away, one longtime Tulsa resident who grew up in the house next door to the Aurandt home posted a wonderful picture on his Web site to accompany his tribute to the broadcaster. It was snapped by his father in 1957. In the photo we see a familiar smiling man in a dress shirt, suspenders, and necktie sitting on a porch swing. His arm is around a weathered but attractive older woman in a stylish polka-dot dress with a lace collar. He looks confidently into the camera. She looks shyly away. It is Paul Harvey sitting on the porch of that old house with his mother.

The place must never have been the same after the heartache of Christmas week 1921. Hundreds of miles away from the nearest family member, Anna was on her own with two children. To make ends meet, she built some apartments behind the house and began to take in boarders, a source of income she maintained right up until her passing in 1960 at the age of seventy-two.

The family's financial straits impacted Paul in interesting ways and tended to color his childhood memories of Tulsa in darker shades. After a 1994 visit to Tulsa in which he returned to many of the landmarks of his early days there, he wrote an essay he called "Homecoming." In it he says:

> Over my shoulder a backward glance.
>
> The world began for Paul Harvey in Tulsa, Oklahoma.
>
> Ever since I have made tomorrow my favorite day. I've been uncomfortable looking back.
>
> My recent revisit reminded me why. The Tulsa I knew isn't there anymore. And the memories of once-upon-a-time are more bitter than sweet.
>
> Of the lawman father I barely knew.
>
> The widowed mother who worked too hard and died too soon. And my sister Frances.
>
> Tulsa was three graves side-by-side.
>
> Recently I came face-to-face with the place where a small Paul Harvey's mother buttoned his britches to his shirt to keep them up and it down.

Tulsa is a copper penny which a small boy from East Fifth Place placed on a trolley track to see it mashed flat.

It's a slingshot made from a forked branch aimed at a living bird and the bird died and he cried and he is still crying.

That little lad was seven when he snapped a rubber band against the neck of the neighbor girl and pretty Ethel Mae Mazelton ran home crying and he, lonely, had wanted only to get her to notice him.

Somehow he blamed Tulsa for the war which took his best friend, Harold Collins . . .

And classmate Fred Markgraff . . . And never gave them back.

In Tulsa, Oklahoma, he learned the wages of sin smoking grapevine behind the garage and getting a mouthful of ants.

Longfellow Elementary School is closed now; dark.

Tulsa High is a business building.

The old house at 1014 is in mourning for the Tulsa that isn't there anymore.

It was in that house that a well-meaning mother arranged a surprise birthday party when he was sixteen; invited his school friends, including delicate Mary Betty French without whom he was sure he could not live.

He hated that party for revealing to her and to them his house, so much more modest than theirs.[8]

That party wasn't the first time he had felt shame about his station in life. In his 1954 book, *Autumn of Liberty*, Paul tells of the day he left school early and then walked sideways, with his back to the buildings, all the way to downtown Tulsa. The reason for this was that the seat of his only pair of trousers had torn during school.

He had called his mother, and she had instructed him to meet her at a downtown department store. There she would take the eleven dollars and ninety-five cents she had been putting aside for taxes and instead purchase Paul a new suit of clothes with two pairs of pants.

But before he reached his mother, the boy of ten battled intense embarrassment and self-consciousness as he slowly made his way down the long mile of blocks between school and that store. And as he watched the fancy cars of Tulsa's upper crust drive by, he felt something new—a rising, agonizing bitterness:

> In that long mile . . . many liveried chauffeurs in their great limousines had passed . . . unmindful of my predicament. But the feeling to a half-frightened, half-ashamed youth was that they knew and didn't care.[9]

That night, one of Paul's favorite teachers from the elementary school happened to be visiting his mother. Paul loved and trusted Miss Harp and took the opportunity to pour out his angry heart to her. The kind teacher may have sensed in Paul's words and emotions the making of a formative, life-altering moment. Or perhaps the hand of Providence, moved by a praying mother, inspired her to say just the right words. In any event, she didn't laugh or dismiss his concerns. As Paul remembered it:

> Miss Harp, in quiet kindness, said something I am sure she never dreamed that boy would write into a nationwide broadcast . . . or into the text of a book. She said, and I recall the words almost exactly . . .
> "Paul, never feel resentment in your heart for those who have more than you. Just do all that you can as long as you live to preserve this last wonderful land . . . in which any man willing to stay on his toes . . . can reach for the stars."[10]

The lesson of that watershed moment never left Paul's soul. He would later say that from then on, he vowed never to be tempted to try to make himself feel bigger by tearing someone else down. "From that day . . . I was never one who sought to make the small man tall by cutting the legs off a giant."[11]

In the meantime, Paul's mother did the best she could for her children, particularly the precocious little boy who had quickly developed a fondness for books, a love of wordplay, and a knack for building "cat's whisker" crystal radio sets out of cigar boxes. Oh, and he had a flair for salesmanship, too. He'd take those radios he built for a quarter and sell them to neighbors for a dollar.

The sounds those radio sets magically pulled out of the air captivated the fatherless little boy. And through the crackling static—behind the tinny voices from unseen places—Paul Harvey Aurandt seems to have heard something others didn't.

It was the sound of destiny calling.

CHAPTER 2

THE VOICE
OF OKLAHOMA

*"When a person prays for guidance, and doors continue
to open instead of close, a person comes to think of his job
as a high obligation . . . to enlighten and inform."*

PAUL HARVEY, TO LARRY KING

TODAY THE SOUTHWEST CORNER OF ADMIRAL PLACE and Sheridan Avenue on Tulsa's east side is occupied by an aging, half-empty, fifties-era strip mall. There is talk of demolishing it.

Back on the last day of September in 1927, the same spot lay beyond the edge of town and was essentially a hay field with a hangar and some navigation lights, the latter enabling it to serve as a private airfield for one of Tulsa's numerous oil barons.

On this day Spartan Field, as most people called it, had attracted a multitude of gawkers. A pair of makeshift rope fences swagged on either side kept the throng from pouring onto the sixty-foot-wide swath cut in the field for a landing strip.

One of the biggest celebrities on the planet was making a quick stop in Tulsa on a nationwide tour, and seemingly everyone was there to get a glimpse. Among them was Paul Aurandt, just a few weeks beyond his ninth birthday. The boy used his combination of small stature and outsize determination to his best advantage, slipping and pushing and squeezing through the crowd until he found himself pressed against the rope with a clear view of the landing strip.

Soon the drone of an engine could be heard in the distance, and a few moments later a gray single-engine airplane descended onto the field and gradually trundled to a stop. It was a Ryan M2 high-wing, heavily modified from the standard configuration to enable long flights without refueling. She had a name painted on her side—*Spirit of St. Louis.*

As Paul would later recall the scene, what he got for his effort was "a glimpse of a lean young man alighting from an old tin goose—Slim Lindbergh. He had flown alone across the Atlantic Ocean and had opened a new and limitless horizon for small boys everywhere."[1]

Like most other Americans, this particular boy had eagerly followed "Lucky Lindy's" quest to be the first person to make a solo, nonstop transatlantic flight. He pored over the newspapers and stayed glued to the radio.

In 1927 commercial radio was still very much in its infancy. The first commercial stations had signed on to the airwaves only in major cities like New York, Detroit, and Chicago in 1920. That year, the Republican National Convention in Chicago was the first one to be broadcast to a large number of Americans over radio. Tulsa's first fledgling radio stations signed on in 1922 but didn't last more than a year or so.

The city's first serious commercial radio endeavor was launched in 1926. A new station with call letters KVOO—the "Voice of Oklahoma"—went on the air in June of that year. Oil magnate W. G. Skelly acquired the station in 1928.

While most stations of that day did their best to emulate the big-city stations back East in both style and content, KVOO very consciously chose to glory in its rural setting. In the late 1920s, the preteen Paul would have heard live studio music from among thirty or more different musical acts that performed at the station each week, including Jimmie Wilson and His Cat Fish String Band and Otto Gray and His Oklahoma Cowboys. A few years later, an aspiring singer and actor got a regular gig on KVOO as Oklahoma's Yodeling Cowboy. His name was Gene Autry, and his appearances on the Tulsa station ultimately caught the ear of Arthur Satherley, a record producer for Sears, Roebuck's Conqueror label. Soon Autry had a regular spot on Sears's Chicago radio station WLS and was on his way to movie and television stardom.

Paul would have also heard popular comedy and variety fare from the big networks such as *Amos 'n' Andy*, *The Jack Benny Program*, and Eddie Cantor. And like other radio-enthralled Americans in the late 1920s, 1930s, and 1940s, he enjoyed dramas such as *The Shadow* and *The Lone Ranger*. Still, it was unapologetically playing to the heartland that made KVOO distinctive, and something about that must have made a deep impression on the future broadcaster. In later years, when Paul was a wildly successful national radio presence in Chicago, he would receive countless offers to move to New York City, the mecca of the broadcasting business and the place to which every media professional was supposed to aspire. He would politely decline every one of the offers.

He was clear about his reasons. He did not want to lose touch with heartland values and the heartland people to whom he knew he was called to speak. At the height of Paul's career, an interviewer asked him why he consistently refused to move to New York. He replied:

> I can't stay back in New York for thirty days and maintain my perspective. I start thinking, like the rest of the Manhattanites, that the sun rises behind the UN building and sets in the Appalachians. Of course, it doesn't.[2]

Like the radio station that captured his imagination as a boy, Paul didn't give a fig about impressing the self-important, being accepted by the beautiful people, or earning the praise of the urbane. The fact is, throughout his professional life, the man with the most-listened-to news voice in America picked and screened the stories he chose to cover using one simple, overriding criterion. As he told a reporter back in 2000:

> I always used to think of my wife's sister, a Missouri farm
> wife. I would always think about Betty before I would decide
> on a broadcast. I may have spent all morning on a piece and
> then ask myself, *"Would Betty understand?"* and maybe more
> importantly, *"Would Betty care?"* I still throw a lot of good stuff
> in the wastebasket because there's no real point in talking over
> the heads of others.[3]

There was another media force shaping the vision and values of young Paul, one that, as with the example of KVOO, reinforced the virtue of speaking plainly to regular people living regular lives. He was a newspaperman who rose to national fame and influence from behind a typewriter in Emporia, Kansas. His name was William Allen White, a friend and adviser to presidents Theodore and Franklin Roosevelt.

White had purchased the *Emporia Gazette* in 1895 and, through his compelling but plainspoken editorials, became one of the most influential national voices of the period between the world wars.

Paul once confided that it was White, the man who came to be known as "the unofficial voice of Middle America," who taught him that it was possible to "embrace a whole world of wisdom without ever leaving Emporia, Kansas." From White's example, he learned never to abandon his own Midwest roots. Paul professed to have been in awe of the man's ability to reduce "the world's complexities to shirt-sleeve English that anybody could comprehend."[4]

This capacity to bring the world and the issues shaping it to the vast, silent center of America must have made a profound impression on young Paul. In turn his voice and gift for oratory must have made an impression on others. One in particular was a very special teacher at Tulsa's Central High School, a woman who changed the history of broadcasting and entertainment, not once but twice.

• • •

Striking in appearance and passionately committed to seeing students develop in the dramatic arts, the speech and drama teacher at Central High would eventually come to be a revered, even legendary, figure in the Tulsa arts scene and indeed throughout Oklahoma. But in 1933, Isabel Ronan was a young, energetic teacher on a mission to expose reluctant students to the genius of Shakespeare and hone the skills of future orators and actors.

Back in those days, students in Miss Ronan's class were likely to study "declamation"—the art of speech making in the big, dramatic style characteristic of politicians and preachers. In the cause of delivering the perfect speech or dramatic reading, students like Paul would have been given elocution exercises to perform. These vocal drills would not only warm up the voice but, more important, train young speakers to enunciate each consonant and syllable distinctly and crisply.

In later decades, anyone privileged to be an observer of a Paul Harvey broadcast was invariably startled when, several minutes before airtime, the well-dressed older man behind the microphone broke into a loud, rapid recitation of "Mee-mee-mee-maw-maw-maw-moo-moo-moo; mee-mee-mee-maw-maw-maw-moo-moo-moo," followed by "Diddle-de-diddle-de-dee; diddle-de-diddle-de-dee," "Ngonga-ngonga-ngonga," and "Wolf-one-two-three-four."

Right up until his final *The Rest of the Story* episode in 2009, he ran through Miss Ronan's elocution drills to prepare himself to speak to 20 million listeners. But the broadcaster owed more than just a distinctive "pause and effect" delivery style to his teacher. Without her, he may never have found a place in radio at all, perhaps following instead the path of his hero in newspapers, William Allen White, deploying his powers of persuasion in insurance sales.

What we know is that Isabel Ronan heard something remarkable in the voice and delivery of that gangly fourteen-year-old freshman named Paul, the one who had lost his father and yet was so poised and confident.

As he later told it, she marched him down to radio station KVOO one afternoon after school and insisted on speaking to the manager.

"This young man ought to be on the radio," she boldly told the man.

Paul recalled that she clearly wasn't prepared to accept no as an answer from either of them. He walked away with permission to come in after school or in the evening and help out around the station. It was unpaid apprentice work only, but he was thrilled to be given the opportunity to be around the newsmen behind the familiar voices and to rub shoulders with the popular musical stars who were a constant presence at the station. Among these were Bob Wills and His Texas Playboys, the group that had essentially invented the genre of western swing from inside KVOO's downtown Tulsa studios.

Recalling those days in an interview, Paul said, "I felt like I was king of the world."[5]

A few years later, Miss Ronan would drag another young student down to those studios with an equally confident declaration. Two grades behind Paul Aurandt at Central High, a skinny Jewish boy named Leonard Rosenberg had shown a flair for acting. He, too, landed a place at the station and went on to bigger things. He pursued acting on radio dramas and ultimately found enormous success in the theater, in movies, and on *The Odd Couple*, one of the most popular television series of all time. After leaving Tulsa, young Leonard Rosenberg changed his name to Tony Randall.

Paul seized his opportunity and, after homework and chores were completed, he headed over to the station every evening to perform any task they would let him tackle. He would sweep up at night, set up the equipment for remote broadcasts, organize the record collections, help write commercial spot copy—something for which he displayed an amazing aptitude—and soon found himself playing his guitar on air and reading short announcements or news items. He proved so valuable that after a year, the manager's conscience compelled him to start paying the young man.

For the remainder of his high school days, Paul was a fixture at KVOO, learning and loving every aspect of the radio business, including selling spots to advertisers and then selling those advertisers' goods or services to listeners. He developed a deep appreciation for the way business and commerce—the connecting of buyers and sellers through markets—created the engine that made America great and strong.

"I can't look down on the commercial sponsors of these broadcasts," he explained in a 1988 interview. "Too often they have very, very important messages to put across. Without advertising, my goodness, we'd still be in this country what Russia mostly still is: a nation of bearded bicyclists with b.o."[6]

In later years Paul would become America's leading champion of business and entrepreneurship and her foremost hopeful romantic about the power of free enterprise to reward hard work and ingenuity with success. He once wrote,

> The economic vehicle we rode to the top is free competitive American capitalism! Do not let the word "Capitalism" frighten you. It has been abused, misused, and maligned and slurred like some naughty word nice people do not use . . . but capitalism has been our good servant. Yet some want to trade a good servant for a bad master.[7]

In those early years in radio, however, he was still just learning how to present himself on the air. Not surprisingly, his instinct was to imitate as faithfully as possible the "pros" who sat behind the microphone all day. So adept did he become at this mimicry, he said people often couldn't tell when the main personality left and Paul took over.

So when did Paul's signature style emerge? As he explained it:

> It was a very crude but gifted program director who one day took me aside and said, "Paul Harvey, as long as you are imitating, the best you can ever hope to be is second best. The only thing you can do better than anybody else is be Paul Harvey." And from then until now, I have merely been trying to be Paul Harvey.[8]

After high school, he enrolled at the University of Tulsa for a time with the intention of studying journalism and literature, but he grew impatient to continue his radio career and soon dropped out. This is understandable. When you have worked at one of the most famous radio stations in the Midwest for three years, the prospect of sitting on the sidelines to absorb book learning must seem unbearable. And unnecessary, since, unlike most of his high school classmates, Paul already knew precisely what he wanted to do with his life and was fully qualified to get a job doing it.

Almost immediately, at the tender age of nineteen, he was offered the opportunity to run his own station in Salina, Kansas. In his characteristic self-deprecating way, he later contended that they hired him to run KFBI precisely because they wanted it to fail. As he reminisced aloud before a group of students and faculty at Kansas State University in 2003:

> A Dr. Brinkley had used his radio station in Abilene to sell young goat glands to old men and he was evicted from the

United States. He fled to Mexico and his station with studios in Abilene and Salina and Milford was bought by Farmers and Bankers Life Insurance Company, and redesignated KFBI, Farmers Bankers Life Insurance. The negotiation moved the station to the company's home base, Wichita, or wanted to, but the FCC was not going to let them make that move. They had to demonstrate that the station couldn't otherwise survive out there in the plains of Kansas. So what they did was to hire the least experienced teenage applicant they could possibly find to help them lose money and that was me. And when I made the station profitable I became disposable, but not before I had become a flag-waving Kansan.[9]

That successful three-year sojourn in Kansas did more than grow Paul's confidence. Something of lasting spiritual significance happened to the young man out there on those rolling plains.

Until they leave home, it is impossible to know whether the faith of kids who grow up in religiously oriented households is owned or merely borrowed from their parents. This is doubly the case for those who grow up in a place like Tulsa, where religious fervor is practically infused in the drinking water along with fluoride.

Indeed, the 1935 Central High School yearbook, the *Tom Tom*, shows Paul, a junior, active in two clubs. He was a leader in the drama club (naturally) and something called the Hi-Y club. That particular page of the yearbook features a group picture with a smiling Paul Aurandt on the back row. It explains that the Hi-Y clubs were an extension of the YMCA and had as their purpose "to create, maintain, and extend the high standards of Christian fellowship throughout the school and community."

Clearly, the Paul of the Tulsa years was moral and God-fearing and outwardly Christian in every respect. But there is reason to believe that his faith at that time was of the borrowed variety. Then, in those Kansas years, he met a group of Mennonite Christians, some of whom traveled to other churches around the state singing as the Norse Gospel Trio. He saw in his new friends a dimension of relationship with God he didn't recognize in himself. He'd memorized the familiar words of John 3:16 from the King James Version as a boy, and now he couldn't stop thinking about them and pondering their meaning: "For God so loved the world, that he gave his only begotten Son, that whosoever believeth in him should not perish, but have everlasting life."

"Sometimes I would get to thinking about that verse—how wonderful it was," he would recall many years later. "I never made it to the altar in any church, but I liked that promise of 'everlasting life.' So one night, alone in my room, kneeling at my bed, I offered my life to Christ."[10]

Standing before those Kansas State students at the age of eighty-five, Paul spoke tenderly of his days at that Salina radio station:

Traveling to Kansas corners with the Norse Gospel Trio from
our radio station to many Mennonite churches in the state,
I learned to love God and country and Kansas. Before you
were born, I was born again in Kansas.

This wasn't the end of Paul's spiritual journey. It was only the beginning of a quest for inward peace and higher meaning that would require another milestone stop and three decades to complete. But it is clear that, before moving on to bigger cities, larger audiences, national acclaim, and great wealth, the talented young man found an anchor for his soul—along with a faith that he owned for himself.

A good thing it was, too. For though he didn't know it at the time, he wasn't too many months distant from meeting the Christian girl who would help make the next seven decades of his life an extraordinary journey of success and happiness. And she probably wouldn't have had him any other way.

CHAPTER 3

BEHIND EVERY SUCCESSFUL MAN . . .

RADIO INK: *When you look back on your career, is there one achievement that you're most proud of?*

PAUL HARVEY: *Of course. Getting the right girl to say "I do"!*

STANDING OUTSIDE THE DOOR OF KXOK STUDIOS in downtown St. Louis, Lynne Cooper looked down at the neatly clipped newspaper ad and read it one more time. She was a little unsure of what kind of reception she was going to get inside. They might not be expecting a "girl."

Sure, she had excelled at nearly everything she had ever tried in her brief twenty-two years on earth. Yes, she was Phi Beta Kappa at Washington University there in St. Louis, which lay only a few miles from her childhood home. Yes, she already had a bachelor's degree in English and was well on her way to earning her master's with honors. And yes, this was ultramodern, progressive 1939—not the Dark Ages. But now she was venturing outside the open-minded, sheltering cocoon of the university. This was radio. And everyone knew radio was a man's world.

Lynne Cooper had been born into a prominent St. Louis family in 1916, the sixth daughter of a respected judge. Early on, her five doting older sisters had given her the nickname Angel, and it had stuck. It was what everyone her entire life had called her. Her mother had passed away when Angel was only nine but not before imparting to her daughter a love for books, an encouragement to write, and a belief that women should be able to do whatever their aptitude and passion draw them to.

In fact, Angel had penned an entire novel when she was only twelve and early on had announced her intention to pursue a career as a writer. Around that time, she told a novelist who was a dinner guest in the Cooper home of her ambitions. He tried to discourage her, painting a grim picture of a writer's life and prospects. But he failed. She was determined that writing, in some form, would be her life's work. And that remained her passion and her plan when the petite, wasp-waisted girl with blonde hair, bright eyes, and a sharp mind entered nearby Washington University and immersed herself in the liberal arts.

Now an ad in the campus newspaper had caught the young graduate student's eye. Radio station KXOK was looking for ideas and concepts for "educational programming." Angel had already spent some time thinking about how the pervasive and powerful medium of radio might be put to better use. Though she didn't know it at the time, Angel had begun thinking like a producer. Now here was a station actually looking for ideas, so she had sent a list of possibilities. She was surprised to receive a message a few days later asking her to come down to the station to discuss her suggestions.

Angel walked through the door, met the station's program director, and walked out with a job. He had been so impressed with her ideas and the confidence with which she had presented them that he decided to put her on the air.

• • •

On her first official day at the station, she had been introduced to a tall, handsome fellow who was also fairly new to the place. The recently arrived roving reporter was presented to Angel as the director of special projects, a title probably created to imply that its holder was "available to do pretty much anything that needs to be done." His name was Paul Aurandt. He stood a trim six feet two; had a thick mane of wavy, reddish blond hair and clear blue eyes; and was stylishly dressed. She noticed he was not a bad-looking fellow.

Paul had come to KXOK from its sister station KOMA in Oklahoma City, a 50,000-watt powerhouse where he had done newscasts and roving reporter work. He had landed back in Oklahoma after having failed to fail at KFBI in Salina.

Of course, the path of promotion for a radio man is invariably a series of moves to bigger cities with larger markets. Thus it was a significant promotion for Paul to move from Salina to Oklahoma City, even though he'd become a station manager right out of high school. Then, when a job at the sister station opened up in St. Louis, he jumped at it.

In later years he would recall with great fondness how in St. Louis, after growing homesick for his Kansas travels with the Norse Gospel Trio, he discovered a black gospel quartet called the Friendly Brothers Four (later, the Friendly Brothers Five) and would visit churches in East St. Louis just to hear them sing.

Paul didn't own a car at that time, so the move would have meant taking a bus out of Oklahoma City up fabled Route 66—also known as the Main Street of America and the Mother Road—with an automatic stop in Tulsa that would have enabled him to look in on his mother. After a brief visit, he would have been back on Route 66 all the way to St. Louis. Had he failed to get off the bus there, he would have ended up in Chicago, the third largest radio market in America. But that step of promotion was still a few years away.

It was an exciting, if sobering, time to be a newsman. In the autumn of 1939, the tinderbox of Europe, fueled by the rise of Hitler's Nazi menace, had just been ignited. The spark had been Germany's invasion of Poland in September of that year. The dogs of war had finally slipped the leash, and the question on everyone's mind was whether FDR would heed the demands of Paul's hero Lindbergh, and fellow "America First"-ers, to keep the United States out of the conflict. Meanwhile, to America's west, a rising, militaristic Japan was making trouble for U.S. interests in the Pacific.

On the day he first spotted his future wife, however, Paul's mind was concentrated on more pleasant domestic matters, specifically, the beautiful coed standing before him.

Instantly smitten, he asked her for a lift to the airport on some flimsy pretext. She obliged, and he found himself a passenger in a white, late-model Nash Lafayette coupe. Around Washington University, Angel Cooper had become so well-known for tearing about at high speeds in that Nash, she had earned herself another nickname—"the Blonde Blizzard."

That airport errand somehow led to dinner together, which, in turn, led to a long, soul-baring chat that evening in Angel's car.

Just how taken with this whip-smart beauty was Paul? Before he got out of the car that night, he asked Angel Cooper to marry him.

Naturally, she didn't say yes right away, but within a year the two were wed in what would turn out to be a historic merger of two enormous media talents in the making. Angel had career aspirations and had no intention of laying them aside just because she had a ring on her finger. But that ambition now extended to her husband, who was currently earning all of $29.50 per week. She planned for the *both* of them to go places.

Her positive influence on her husband's career began almost immediately. As Paul recalled to Larry King in 1988, "Angel decided she wanted to be married to a network news commentator. And she is the one who gave our lives direction."[1]

It is easy to miss the significance of the three words in that term *network news commentator*. In those days before television, there were three very distinct tiers of responsibility for radio newsmen at both the local and network levels. Those just starting out in radio news were assigned the designation of reporter. After some years and demonstrated skill, a reporter might become a news analyst and be given the opportunity to file more in-depth reports on certain issues. Only a few of these earned a promotion to the designation as news commentator. The commentators were given the opportunity to express their own views and opinions in the same way that writers for a newspaper's op-ed page would.

So when Angel told her husband she wanted to be married to a network news commentator, she was describing a very specific, very ambitious target. It was one that would necessarily narrow and focus Paul's choices in the future.

Up to that point, he had clearly wanted to sample everything the wide, wild world of radio could offer. And he had. There were a number of ways to make a living in radio besides being a newsman, including playing music as a disc jockey, performing in dramas or comedies, writing, managing, producing, or even selling. At this juncture in Paul Harvey's career, it was not at all clear which path he was ultimately going to take. But Angel quickly sized up her man's gifts—a commanding voice, a distinctive delivery, a gift for wordsmithery, and perhaps most significant, a principled passion for America and her people—and knew precisely where he was destined to have the greatest success.

He wisely deferred to Angel's instincts on career decisions. In his words: "Later, when other offers would come along . . . acting, politics, et cetera . . . it was Angel who would analyze the offer. . . . 'Is this advancement or is this a digression?' If it was a digression, she'd say 'no.'"[2]

By the way, that white Nash coupe? When Angel passed away on May 3, 2008, at the age of ninety-two, it was sitting in the garage of Reveille Ranch, the Harveys' Missouri farm home on the banks of the Mississippi River. Through the decades, neither of them could ever bear to think of parting with the vehicle that had been the venue for their first hours together and the setting for Paul's impulsive first-date proposal.

Love, however, has never been able to keep history from marching relentlessly forward. So by the time of the Harveys' June 1940 wedding, Winston Churchill's pleas to FDR for more substantial American help in surviving the Nazi blitz were getting more persuasive, and tensions with the Japanese empire were rising rapidly in the Pacific.

When newlywed Paul got an opportunity to go to Hawaii for a few months to cover the deployment and movement of the U.S. naval fleet in the Pacific, Angel encouraged him to take it. For her part, she would take a job at a Tulsa radio station, where she could be close to Paul's mom and hone her broadcasting skills. She didn't know the half of it.

Not long after arriving at the CBS affiliate in Tulsa, Angel ended up running an entire daily shift by herself. From 4:00 p.m. to midnight each weekday, she spun records, announced, and did all the news and weather breaks. In other words, she got a crash course in attracting and holding a radio audience.

In early December of 1941, Paul's Hawaii assignment drew to a close as tensions between the United States and Japan reached the breaking point. In fact, as he was making his way back home by ship and train, the Japanese attacked Pearl Harbor and pulled America into World War II.

The boy who had thrilled to Lindbergh's exploits never lost his fascination with flying. Furthermore, after Pearl Harbor, Slim Lindbergh—the high-profile isolationist champion of the effort to keep America out of the war—had quickly enlisted in the Army Air Force and had become a key consultant to its leadership.

At some point shortly after his return home, the twenty-three-year-old Paul signed up for, and was accepted into, a program called the Army Air Force Air Cadets. It is a bitter irony that this decision—born of a love for country and a childhood dream of learning to fly—would end up creating confusion and hurtful accusations about Paul's military service decades later during the bitter intracultural fights over the Cold War and Vietnam.

During World War II, the Air Force was a division of the United States Army. Rapid expansion of the Army Air Forces (AAF) just preceding and immediately following the attack on Pearl Harbor created a huge demand for qualified pilots. There was just one problem. Only so many pilots could be trained at any one time. There was a limited number of training aircraft and instructors. At the same time, the horrific mortality rate for pilots meant that a steady stream of trained fliers was needed. More than 193,000 new pilots entered the AAF during World War II. Meanwhile another 124,000 candidates failed at some point during training or were killed in accidents.[3]

This created a significant logistical dilemma for the army. How could this very specialized branch of service keep a pool of qualified candidates at the ready without losing them to the draft or to enlistment in other branches of the military?

Their answer was the Aviation Cadet program for which Paul eagerly signed up. It created a reservoir of qualified pilot-trainees-in-waiting—removing them from the draft pool and "locking them up" for the exclusive use of the AAF until they could be called to active duty.

For the first two years of America's involvement in World War II, Paul would stand by in this state of limbo: expecting to be called up to start pilot training at any moment but needing to stay busy and earn a living in the meantime. In this season, Paul and Angel took radio jobs in towns with sonorous American names like Missoula, Montana, and Kalamazoo, Michigan. They saw the war from the vantage point of small town USA, and this further connected the broadcaster to what coastal elites and snobs would one day derisively label "flyover country."

The couple found another important use for this waiting period. If they were going to realize their dream of seeing Paul become a network news commentator, he was going to have to broaden his education and deepen his understanding of some complex issues. Yes, his Tulsa upbringing had infused him with a visceral conservatism; he had "studied, long-distance, at the feet of publisher William Allen White" as a young man; and his spiritual awakening in the Kansas years had solidified the bearing of his strong moral compass. But they knew this wasn't enough. In his words:

> I needed to build an intellectual base for our goals. Marrying a Phi Beta Kappa key with a master's degree in English helped. But I had to do a lot of homework myself.[4]

With Angel's academic background in literature to guide him, he read many of the "great books" of Western civilization. He also feasted on Adam Smith's *The Wealth of Nations*, Edward Gibbon's *The Decline and Fall of the Roman Empire*, Oswald Spengler's *The Decline of the West*, and numerous critiques of socialism, fascism, and communism.

In other words, Paul supplemented his year at the University of Tulsa with a rigorous self-education. The result was a flowering and solidifying of his philosophy—a worldview that prized liberty, self-reliance, self-government, and moral virtue as keys to American strength and longevity. These values overlaid, rather than displaced, the instinctive isolationism he had absorbed from Charles Lindbergh and the deep-rooted spiritual pacifism of his Anabaptist background. In the decades to follow, all of these would emerge as consistent themes in Paul Harvey's views on the news.

Finally, in December of 1943, as victory in Europe seemed increasingly assured and the tide seemed to be turning in the Pacific, Paul got the telegram he'd been expecting for almost two years. He'd been called up and was finally going to don a uniform and get behind the stick of an airplane.

Then, almost immediately, his hopes were dashed. By 1944 that pool of waiting pilots in the cadet reserves had become a surplus.

No sooner had his pilot training begun than he learned that 24,000 cadets were being transferred to the army ground forces for retraining as infantry and that he was among them. The infantry! His cherished dreams of flying came crashing to earth.

Three months later, according to army records, Paul suffered a heel injury in a training accident on an obstacle course and was discharged.

Sadly, this bizarre sequence of events—the long wait to be called up, then the unexpected reassignment to infantry training, followed by the injury-related discharge after only three months—would be easily misunderstood, misinterpreted, and mischaracterized. This indeed happened decades later when Paul was a rising voice for patriotism in an era when unabashed love for country was growing unfashionable.

In a foreshadowing of the "chicken hawk" smear that would become popular with the antiwar Left during the administration of George W. Bush, a 1978 profile of Paul in *Esquire* magazine tried to paint the promilitary broadcaster as a coward and hypocrite. The cover featured a grotesque caricature of Paul's head atop an eagle, mimicking the Great Seal of the United States. But instead of grasping an olive branch and arrows in its talons, this cartoon eagle clutched a microphone and golf clubs in one claw, and a wad of cash in the other. The article portrayed him as having avoided military service as long as possible and then feigning mental illness in order to get a quick, though dishonorable, discharge. The magazine's teaser synopsis of the article sneered:

> This balding, blue-eyed, blustering broadcaster may be the richest newsman in the country bar none. But the cornflakes-and-corn-bread character Paul Harvey presents to listeners is largely false.[5]

Tellingly, it was *Esquire*'s hit piece that turned out to be largely false. Paul angrily disputed the allegations, and later an official army spokesman informed inquiring reporters that the story was inaccurate on virtually every damaging detail. *Esquire* never issued a correction. And it wasn't the first or the last time that a Left-leaning journalist would try to take down the man whose voice of common sense and traditional values was heard by more people every day than any other in America.

Paul eventually did realize his dreams of flight. As soon as the couple had the financial resources to make it possible, he became a private pilot, got a multiengine rating, and flew well into his seventh decade. He was a member of AOPA, the Aircraft Owners and Pilots Association, for more than fifty years, as well as a member of the Experimental Aircraft Association.

With Paul's discharge in March of 1944, he and Angel contemplated their futures. Paul wanted to make another run at becoming an Army Air Force pilot, but they had more fliers than they needed. Angel believed they could both get radio jobs in a large market where they could report on the biggest story of the twentieth century—the war—and start exposing a wider audience to Paul's talents as a newsman. Her husband had mixed emotions about that plan. One of them, he frankly admitted, was *fear*.

There was a lot about life in places like Missoula, Salina, and Kalamazoo that Paul found deeply appealing. And he loved the self-reliance and community spirit of rural Americans. But in his heart he knew he could never be fulfilled reporting on city council meetings and zoning board controversies. He felt a powerful call to be a part of the national fight to preserve that American goodness he prized in those small towns. It was a goodness he viewed as the fountainhead of America's strength and prosperity.

Both he and Angel sensed he was destined for bigger things. And such things were about to come their way—in poet Carl Sandburg's "City of the Big Shoulders."

CHAPTER 4

A WIDE-ANGLE VIEW OF AMERICA

"You'd better be right . . . because you sound like God."

COMEDIAN DANNY THOMAS, TO PAUL HARVEY

DRIVING UP ROUTE 66 FROM ST. LOUIS TO CHICAGO in that white Nash coupe must have been a giddy and surreal experience for Paul and Angel. Frustrating, too. It was early June of 1944, and the couple surely followed news reports of the long-awaited Allied invasion of France along the way. D-day had finally come just days earlier on June 6. Here was the biggest news story to come out of the war since Pearl Harbor, and Paul wasn't behind a microphone.

It was indeed an extraordinary time to be in the news business. The world seemed to be producing more news than could possibly be gathered, digested, and reported. And Americans had never been so tightly glued to their radios—hungry for every bit of information they could get but also in powerful need of the escape provided by entertainment programs. Now, in this setting, the newsman who had spent most of his professional life as a roving reporter in small, heartland towns was getting his own newscast on a highly rated station in America's third-largest city. It was surely a heady and bracing prospect.

Though the couple must have previously driven near Chicago on the way to the job in Kalamazoo, this day the young man who was apprehensive about big cities would be driving into the heart of one of the most impressive and awe-inspiring skylines of that day.

New York City may have perfected the skyscraper, but Chicago had invented it. Architect William LeBaron Jenney first figured out how to give a building a skeleton of steel rather than of wood or brick, and then he designed the ten-story Home Insurance Building on the corner of the Windy City's LaSalle and Adams streets. Completed in 1885, it was a wonder of the time, and in the decades that followed, Chicago architects built higher and higher.

As Paul and Angel approached downtown, Route 66 would have joined Ogden Avenue running northwest, roughly parallel to the south branch of the Chicago River. Then, as the imposing buildings loomed larger, U.S. 66 would have turned due west on Jackson Boulevard and into the Loop—that famous rectangular circuit of elevated train track that defines Chicago's central business district. There, scattered along the shining arc of lakeshore, they would have seen the thirty-story Wrigley Building (1924); the neo-Gothic spires and buttresses of the thirty-six-story Tribune Tower (1925); the forty-four-story art deco masterpiece Chicago Board of Trade building (1930); and eventually the hulking twenty-five-story Merchandise Mart (1930), near where the Chicago River connects to Lake Michigan.

The city was a sight that never stopped inspiring awe and appreciation in this couple. In fact, a full fifty years beyond this day of arrival, Paul told an audience:

All these years, my family and I do not remember even one time that we have returned from wherever to The Loop, when Angel has looked at our skyline without saying these same words: "Isn't it . . . wonderful?"[1]

Nestled inside the Merchandise Mart building were the studios of WENR, AM 800—an affiliate of NBC's Blue Network that would shortly be sold off to become the ABC network. This 50,000-watt giant was about to introduce Paul Harvey to Chicago. A mutual love affair would ensue, and neither the city nor the man would ever be the same.

• • •

In the beginning, this opportunity for Paul is officially only a temporary one. Popular newsman and commentator Hilmar Robert Baukhage wants to take the summer off, so Paul is hired as a fill-in.

At this time, H. R. Baukhage is already a bit of a legend in radio news circles. It was his reporting from Berlin in 1939 that brought Americans the first news of the start of World War II. And on December 7, 1941, it was Baukhage who aired the first live newscast from the White House for NBC with a marathon eight-hour report on the Pearl Harbor attack. His signature sign-on has always been "Baukhage talking!" and now that distinctive catchphrase serves as the title of his daily noontime Chicago newscast.

You can say that Paul owed this big break to heat and humidity. If you have ever been to Chicago in July or August, you'll understand why, before the era of widespread air-conditioning, it wasn't unusual for newsmen with enough corporate clout to slip away from Chicago for a couple of months. This was even more the case in Washington, D.C., which had been constructed on a giant swampy tidal basin. Prior to the 1960s, our nation's capital became a virtual ghost town every summer.

For the balance of the summer, Paul will host the daily fifteen-minute *Baukhage Talking* newscast, and Angel will produce it. It is a division of labor that will serve them very well for the next six decades. By the way, this is the point in his career at which he will permanently drop his surname from his on-air work. He was still Paul Aurandt at some of the smaller station jobs in previous years. From this point forward, he is always and only "Paul Harvey."

Using one's middle name as an on-air surname is a time-honored practice in the radio business. Furthermore, Paul is tired of spelling his name out for everyone he meets. He and Angel also suspect that listeners might be reluctant to write in to the station if they are unsure about how to spell the name of the newscaster they have just heard. And the couple definitely wants people to write in. They are counting on this temporary opportunity becoming a permanent one.

June 20, 1944, is the first day the name Paul Harvey ever appears in the *Chicago Tribune*'s radio program listings. There is big war news to report this day too.

Some of it is good: The U.S. Navy has dealt a heavy blow to the Japanese, particularly their naval air fleet, in the Battle of the Philippine Sea. U.S. losses are relatively small, while the incapacitated Japanese fleet is forced to retreat to Okinawa.

Some of it is not: London reports hits from fifteen examples of Germany's new secret weapon—a rocket-propelled bomb called the V-1. Britain's traditional antiaircraft defenses aren't much use against these supersonic projectiles. Though fast, these bombs are highly inaccurate, and thus civilians are just as likely as military targets to be on the receiving end of these attacks.

What Chicago listeners of WENR hear from this newcomer likely reflects much of what Americans in later decades will come to know as Paul's signature style. The fast pace, the superb writing, the playful way with words, and the mixing in of humor and human interest stories that lighten the heaviness of the negative news are all there. And what about the pauses? Those amazingly . . . long . . . pregnant . . . pauses that will so characterize Paul's delivery for several genera-tions of Americans? They are present as well. Not only do they serve to add drama and keep the listener hanging on every word, they serve a practical purpose. These are live broadcasts, often with live commercial spots, and they must end precisely when the official clock's second hand hits twelve. Paul once professed that the pauses began simply as "a lazy broadcaster's way of ending exactly on time."[2]

Although he always claimed his style was simply him doing his best to "be Paul Harvey," astute listeners couldn't help but notice the influence of one of the most famous sports commentators of the day—Bill Stern.

Stern had pioneered live sports coverage on the radio in the 1930s. His popular daily sports show, *Colgate Sports Newsreel*, had elements that any regular listener of *Paul Harvey News and Comment* in the 1990s would find familiar. Stern broke up the segments of his program into what he called "reels." After the first commercial break he would begin by saying, "Reel Two!" This is clearly a forerunner of Paul's famous "Page Two" lead-in to the first commercial break. Stern was a wonderful storyteller; in fact, he became an actor with a star on the Hollywood Walk of Fame. As such, he had a popular regular feature in which he would dramatically tell some obscure backstory of a famous athlete and not reveal the name until the very end. Again, Paul's popular *The Rest of the Story* would eventually take this raw concept and develop it into a high art form.

• • •

Whatever the management at WENR heard, they liked it. And so did other listening ears around Chicago. The buzz was overwhelmingly positive. Before the summer ended, Paul and Angel's hopes of being offered a permanent position were realized.

When WENR approached the couple about building an additional fifteen-minute Chicago newscast around them, Angel put forth the idea of a 10:00 p.m. program. At that time, WENR was airing a classical music show called *Symphonette with Maestro Piastro*, sponsored by the Longines watch company. Older readers will remember a series of record albums based on these broadcasts titled *Longines Symphonette*. Angel thought there would be a market for a program that brought listeners a summary of the day's news just before most people headed off to bed. The management liked the idea and found a sponsor in the Olian Advertising Agency. Angel was hired as producer and general manager of the show.

Almost overnight, *Paul Harvey News* became the top-rated program for that hour and eventually one of the highest-rated Chicago news programs of any hour. Today many broadcasting historians trace the near-universal tradition of having television news at 10:00 p.m. central daylight time to Angel's original insight with this program.

Paul's success in that time slot was not due to the strength of the program alone. Some pretty savvy self-marketing and promotion was immediately put in place to jump-start the broadcast's listenership and put him on the community's radar screens. Having secured a place on the schedule, he put himself forward to speak to any group or club that would have him. A search of the *Chicago Tribune* archives produces dozens of headlines along the lines of "Libertyville Women to Hear Paul Harvey" and scores of news items like this one:

> The Englewood Woman's club will hold morning and afternoon sessions tomorrow in its clubrooms. . . . At 10:45 a.m. Mrs. John W. Malcolm, public affairs chairman, will present Mrs. Warner D. Burnett who will show Sarah Hackett Stevenson Memorial movies, with Paul Harvey as narrator.[3]

It becomes clear from reading these numerous newspaper mentions that no event was too small and no organization too obscure for Paul to show up and say a few inspiring words. It was a brilliant strategy. And it was in perfect harmony with his lifelong advocacy of the virtues of hard work, self-reliance, and personal initiative. When he extolled America as a land of opportunity in which anyone willing to work a little harder than the next guy and go the extra mile could succeed, he wasn't just spouting theoretical platitudes. It was something he believed and lived.

This consistent grassroots elbow rubbing also connected him with the concerns, views, and interests of regular Chicagoans. As a newcomer, he found in these interactions a shortcut to learning what folks outside the concrete towers were thinking and saying. The lessons he had learned from his journalistic hero, William Allen White, were not lost along Route 66.

Just how popular and influential this fresh young voice had grown in less than a year's time became evident to the management of WENR in April of the following year. On the twelfth, with a successful conclusion to the war on both fronts seemingly within reach, the only president many Americans could remember occupying the White House collapsed suddenly of a cerebral hemorrhage. FDR was dead.

The next night, Paul dedicated his entire broadcast to Roosevelt. He titled the program "A Great Tree Has Fallen and Left an Empty Place against the Sky." It was a touching narrative told from the point of view of FDR's beloved Scottish terrier, Fala. Sixty-four years later at Paul Harvey's funeral service, his son repeated the title of this program to characterize the void left by the passing of his father.

This sentimental tribute to FDR generated the greatest outpouring of response the station had ever seen. Over the following three days, hundreds of listeners wrote in to request a written transcript of the program, and many others called the station to express how much it had moved them.

Recalling that special program in an interview decades later, Paul said:

I was on just one station in those days in Chicago, yet it was an avalanche. I forget the thousands of pieces of mail [we received] in the next three days, but it was unprecedented for any one station to get that much mail on one broadcast. Most of it was people wanting copies; a lot of it was people sharing our tears.[4]

It is noteworthy that the writer of this moving tribute was an opponent of most of FDR's domestic policies. He passionately disagreed with the four-term president's political philosophy on almost every point. And yet he, like many Republican-leaning journalists of that generation, understood that in a time of war it was vital to keep the nation unified and to give the commander in chief as much support as possible. It is an ethic that Paul was to see progressively diminish among his younger news media colleagues over the decades and essentially vanish by the time of his death.

Yes, when it came time to help his listeners say good-bye to the president who had led them through the fierce trials of the Depression and a global war, he had the class and grace to mourn with them rather than throw stones or even present a "balanced" view of the man. In a 1988 interview with Larry King, Paul talked of FDR's passing, how he had indeed disagreed with the president about so many things, yet he then went on to say, "But we were all shocked and very saddened. Part of me thought he would always be my president."

• • •

Later that year, as the German surrender in Europe brought the war in that theater to a close, an additional broadcasting opportunity dropped into Paul's lap. The CBS affiliate in Chicago, WBBM, had an idea for a weekend radio program that would connect returning soldiers to job openings.

In just the first few months after Victory in Europe Day (VE Day), it had become painfully apparent that many discharged servicemen were going to have difficulty finding suitable work. A lot of these guys had been eighteen- and nineteen-year-old boys when they enlisted in 1941. Four years later they were returning battle-hardened men but without ever having held anything other than an after-school job.

The *Jobs for GI Joes* program was probably conceived more as something to help the station fulfill its FCC-mandated quota of public service programming hours than as a vehicle to attract a big audience. Tellingly, it was scheduled when most public service–oriented programming got stuck—on Sunday.

In his first year in Chicago, Paul had already positioned himself as both a patriot and a champion of the regular guy. So he naturally came to mind when the station started looking for a host. Paul loved the idea and, with WENR's permission, seized the offer.

Although it was unusual for a radio personality from one station to host a show on a competing outlet, it wasn't completely unheard of in those days. Frankly, WENR probably agreed to the crossover because the concept for the show sounded like little more than glorified want ads read over the air, and considered it no threat. But this is Paul and Angel Harvey we're talking about.

What WBBM got was a well-written, tightly produced Sunday night show that told the stories of returning Chicagoland soldiers in compelling ways and also featured musical guests and appearances by local and visiting celebrities. The show not only did a surprisingly good job of getting local businesses to create job openings for returning vets but also became a ratings hit.

It bought Paul a mountain of goodwill with veterans' organizations too. On October 7, *Chicago Tribune* readers found this item in their morning papers:

PAUL HARVEY TO RECEIVE DISABLED VETERANS' AWARD
Paul Harvey, conductor of the Jobs for GI Joes program,
will receive a certificate for outstanding service from the
organization of Disabled American Veterans for aid given
veterans of this war during the broadcast of 10:30 o'clock
tonight over WBBM.[5]

All of this attention and profile elevation only increased demand for
Paul as a public speaker. In fact, he signed on with one of the leading
speakers' bureaus of the day, the Redpath Bureau, a few months later.
The flyer that Redpath created to sell Paul as a speaker proclaimed:

Paul Harvey is one of the most dynamic personalities in Radio,
and is one of Redpath's new lecture stars.

He has the highest news rating of any Chicago-originated
commentary. According to the Hooper rating, 26% of all sets
in use at 10 P.M. each night are tuned to Paul Harvey. His
station is WENR. This is phenomenal. Saturday and Sunday
mornings he is a featured news analyst over the ABC network.
Paul Harvey is an exceptionally good speaker with a fine sense
of humor.

The flyer went on to mention the topics of the speeches Paul was
available to deliver. They included "Radio and Peace"; "Let's Talk
Television—Let's Keep Radio Clean"; "Slips That Pass in the Mike";
and "Questions and Answers on Current Problems."

An overeager copywriter at Redpath did take some liberties in
punching up the broadcaster's biography. The promotional brochure
has Paul flying bombers in the South Pacific during World War II.
And it managed to transform Paul's special recognition from the
Disabled American Veterans for his radio program into full-fledged
membership in the organization.

There is no reason to believe Paul was aware of this biographical hyperbole in these flyers until well after they were printed and sent out, if he ever saw them at all. What is clear is that after only eighteen months in one of the largest, most competitive radio markets in America, Paul was a rising star. It is also clear that he and Angel loved Chicago. He was beginning to view his hometown as what he called "the hub of the wheel," with the glamorous, self-important centers of New York, Washington, and Los Angeles at the far edges.

He claimed Chicago gave him a "wide-angle view" of America simply not available from either coast. For the next five years he would enjoy that view while his voice was rarely heard outside the footprint of WENR's signal. He was a star, but only in Chicago. This was soon to change, though—along with the future of radio broadcasting—when Paul had an unlikely encounter with a future Democratic president's father.

CHAPTER 5

MY GOD,
MY COUNTRY,
MYSELF

"My job is to make what is important, interesting.
And what is interesting, important."

PAUL HARVEY

TURNING NORTH UP BEAUTIFUL LAKE SHORE DRIVE, Paul Harvey
drops his car into third gear and turns up the radio to hear what the
boys are talking about this morning. Looking off to his right, he sees
the first bits of morning sun peek above Lake Michigan and reflect
brilliantly off the water.

Paul's own live newscast doesn't air until 10:00 p.m. tonight.
He and Angel won't begin preparation for the broadcast until after
five. But he is regularly invited to be a guest on the local morning
radio shows, and that usually means rolling away from their apart-
ment at 3400 South Lake Shore Drive at sunrise. It makes for a long
day, but the man whose work ethic is rapidly becoming legendary
doesn't mind.

His commute is short but spectacular. Right after the war, Lake
Shore Drive became Chicago's first expressway. Paul's trip of less
than three miles along the lake takes him north past the impressive remnants of Chicago's 1933 World's Fair (A Century of Progress

Exposition); then the city's famous Field Museum; legendary Soldier Field; and "Chicago's front yard," Grant Park. If Paul could see into the future, he would learn that in twenty years—almost to the week— Grant Park would become a battlefield between police and protestors at the 1968 Democratic National Convention and that he would be sharing his perspective on the event with the entire nation.

If that scene would have seemed unthinkable to the Midwestern newsman in 1948, how much more so the fact that in sixty years and a few weeks from this fine morning, a South Side Chicago politician whose absentee father was a black Kenyan would be standing before an ecstatic throng in this same Grant Park declaring victory in the race for the presidency of the United States. Would it have surprised him to learn that he would live to see both events?

On this morning, just as Navy Pier comes into view, Paul turns left on Wacker Drive, travels parallel to the Chicago River for several blocks, and then turns right across the picturesque Franklin Street Bridge to arrive immediately at the mammoth Merchandise Mart building, home of WENR.

He parks, gets out of the car, looks at his reflection in the car window, and straightens his jacket and tie. He's about to tell the city of Chicago "Good day!" And he means it.

• • •

Those years immediately following the war were an extraordinary time to be alive and young in America. The long-running, over-lapping crises of the Great Depression and World War II had made it easy for people of Paul Harvey's generation to think that the grim clouds of austerity and hardship might never clear. But they did.

The sun came out, the boys came home, and America boomed. In 1940, only 44 percent of Americans owned their own homes. Over the next decade or so, that figure would surge to more than

66 percent. In model-year 1945 only seven hundred new cars were produced for the entire nation. It took a couple of years to retool the factories, but by 1949, Detroit was making 5 million new cars—and selling every one of them to eager buyers.

New modern wonders seemed to be emerging on an almost daily basis. Synthetic rubber for tires, Tupperware, aluminum foil, and countless other recent innovations were being converted into the low-cost goods now filling long-barren store shelves. The technological swords forged in the furnace of war were rapidly being beaten into plowshares to improve and enrich the lives of middle-American households.

However, none of these newly affordable consumer innovations would have a greater impact than television. There had been some limited broadcasting of television programming in major cities just prior to the war, though television sets were prohibitively expensive and therefore rarely seen in homes. Virtually all TV broadcasting in the United States had ceased during the war.

Now the boom was on. Most of the big radio stations in major cities rushed to get into the television business as well. WENR in Chicago was no exception.

On September 17, 1948, WENR-TV channel 7 hit the airwaves as an affiliate of the brand-new ABC television network. The first broadcast was a live extravaganza designed to grab as much attention for the new station as possible—and WENR's management made sure its young radio star, Paul Harvey, was part of the event. That morning's newspaper gave the details:

> Several grade A attractions have been lined up by WENR-TV for its opening telecast over channel 7 tonight. They include Victor Borge, Ginny Simms, Jerry Colonna, and Paul Whiteman, who will conduct a 60-piece orchestra in George Gershwin's "Rhapsody in Blue."

Mayor Kennelly, Lt. Gov. Cross, and officials of ABC . . .
will contribute to this ceremony. WENR personalities including
Paul Harvey, Beulah Karney, Herbie Mintz . . . will join in this
portion of the show.[1]

Paul would be a frequent face on Channel 7 over the next few
years. But it was still his voice that was winning him fans and
admirers across the city. In fact, there is evidence the handsome bari-
tone with homespun humor and quick wit was becoming a bit of a
heartthrob.

The *Tribune's* entertainment gossip column, The Tower Ticker,
featured this item a few months after Paul's TV debut:

> RADIO: WENR received a fan letter which makes more
> sense than most. "Dear sirs: My wife, despite the fact that
> her hair needs fixing, the baby needs attention, and I need
> breakfast, can't tear herself away from Paul Harvey and Skip
> Farrell on the radio in the morning. To disillusion her, please
> send photos of Harvey and Farrell to Madelyn Wehbey for
> the benefit of her tired old husband, M.T. Wehbey."[2]

The distressed Mr. Wehbey seemed to think that popular singer
Skip Farrell and Paul wouldn't seem as attractive in reality as they
sounded in Mrs. Wehbey's imagination.

Another popular *Tribune* column quoted Paul on a regular basis.
The Radio Gag Bag, "culled by Larry Wolters," was a sampling
of some of the funniest one-liners and bits heard on national and
Chicago radio shows the previous day. A typical example appearing
on February 5, 1950, repeated jokes heard from the likes of Fibber
McGee and Molly, Groucho Marx, Edgar Bergen with Mortimer
Snerd, and Bob Hope with Doris Day, and it repeated this bit of
interaction from Red Skelton's show:

ROD O'CONNER: Why you don't even understand opera.

RED SKELTON: Who does? One time Lauritz Melchior sang three pages of the Brown Derby menu and no one knew the difference. It's the first time people applauded the fact that a second cup of coffee was free.

That same column made a practice of passing along Paul's word-play witticisms. On this day, a cartoon caricature of the broadcaster, emphasizing his high forehead and depicting him behind a microphone, is followed by:

If the national debt gets much larger, says Paul Harvey, President Truman is going to have to begin his speeches, "Fellow deficitizens . . ."

The previous Christmas, another newspaper column reported on the themes Chicago's high-profile media celebrities had chosen for their Christmas cards that year. The piece noted that the Harveys, "as in other years, have sent out the same greeting—a card with the 23rd Psalm inscribed." The article also noted that a number of the "air notables," as it called the radio celebs, had chosen to send out CARE packages in their friends' names in lieu of cards for 1948. This served as a reminder that, though the United States emerged from the war wholly intact, much of Europe was still smoldering rubble and its people still suffering.

The Marshall Plan—the monumental $13 billion U.S. effort to deliver economic and technical assistance for rebuilding Western Europe—had been underway for about eighteen months, but progress was slow. Widespread starvation was a very real prospect in those bitterly cold winters that followed the war. The Cooperative for American Remittances to Europe (CARE) had been formed in 1945 to give Americans a way to ease suffering across the Atlantic.

To Paul, both programs were shining examples of the inherent goodness of America and of her people. He didn't just believe in America. He believed in believing in America. As he declared in a 1960 recording titled "The Testing Time":

> *I think it has to do with a basic American's creed. Perhaps it never passed the pioneers' lips in this form, but if it had I think it would have gone something like this: "I believe in my God. In my country. And in myself." I know that sounds like a trite, too-simple thing to say, yet it's a rare man today who will dare to stand up and say, "I believe in my God and my country and in myself." And in that order.*

As for faith in God, 1949 found Paul leaning heavily on his. In that year, he and Angel were thrilled to discover they were expecting their first child. Though he never spoke much about their most private matters publicly, Paul did mention in a few interviews that he came close to losing Angel during a difficult delivery. It ultimately required quick work by some of Chicago's finest surgeons to preserve the lives of both mother and infant. Once, late in his life, when responding to the question "What is the hardest story you ever had to cover?" Paul replied:

> The most important story I ever did from a personal point of view was the birth of my son, which was not an easy birth. There were days when his mother's prospects were marginal, so that was a critical experience personally.[3]

Mother and baby eventually came through well and whole. The Aurandts had a son. They named him Paul Harvey Aurandt Jr. but before long had given him the affectionate nickname "Small Paul" or sometimes "Hoppy," a nod to the admired Western movie character Hopalong Cassidy. As the boy grew older, he eventually came to be "Young Paul" to the Harveys and to everyone who knew them.

Paul Jr. practically grew up in Chicago radio newsrooms, accompanying his parents to work whenever he wasn't attending school or practicing the piano. There is a great picture in the ABC Radio Network archives of the three of them sometime in the early 1950s. Young Paul seems to be about four years old. All three are seated around a large newsroom desk, and each is hard at work behind a manual typewriter.

In his youth, Young Paul would prepare for a career as a concert pianist, but he would eventually find the gravitational pull of the family business too compelling. The day would come when the tightly knit trio around the news desk in that black-and-white photo would become the first and only family to have three members inducted into the National Radio Hall of Fame. Eventually, to avoid confusing a world that had come to know his father as "Paul Harvey," Young Paul altered his own public name to Paul Harvey Jr.

It is impossible to overstate how close this family was or how blurry the line between home life and work remained. Paul once told a friend, "Since the first day of our marriage, we've worked side by side. I think that if we had not worked so closely the marriage would not have survived. There has never been the opportunity for neglect."[4]

In 2002, after the signing of that $100 million contract, their longtime friend Rick Kogan, referring to the fact that the Harveys rose at 3:00 a.m., dined at 4:30 p.m., and usually retired after an hour of television by 8:00 p.m., wrote:

> His constant companion . . . has been his wife. They are bound together, personally and professionally, as tightly as seems possible. Since their schedule precludes the sort of social events that help contribute to making a wide circle of friends—who has dinner parties at 4:30 p.m.?—they are closer in ways that

most married couples cannot even imagine. . . . They care for each other in palpable ways, holding hands in public, calling each other "sweetie" and "dear." Close your eyes when around them and you might think you were in the presence of a couple of love-struck teens.[5]

After Angel's death in 2008, Bruce DuMont, president of the Museum of Broadcast Communications and a dear personal friend of the Harveys, said, "[Angel] crafted the most successful radio career of all time. She was to Paul Harvey what Col. Parker was to Elvis Presley." He described the Harveys' relationship as "probably the greatest love story that I've ever experienced."[6]

The amazing symbiotic personal-professional dynamic between husband and wife makes it unthinkable that either of these extraordinarily gifted individuals would have achieved remotely as much had the other one not been present. Thus, if that troubled labor and delivery had resulted in a less happy outcome, there is little doubt that few people outside of Chicago would have ever heard of Paul Harvey.

When an aged Paul whispered to Larry King in 2003, "She is my life," he meant it.

While he almost lost his wife in 1949, Angel came frighteningly close to losing her husband the very next year. The next-to-last paragraph of an August 7, 1950, newspaper item summarizing the previous day's noteworthy auto accidents reported:

Paul Harvey, American Broadcasting Company news broadcaster in Chicago, seriously injured Saturday when his auto overturned in a ditch near Litchfield, Montgomery County. Harvey fell asleep while driving to his farm south of St. Louis to celebrate his 10th wedding anniversary with his wife, Lynn [sic].[7]

Apparently the couple had planned to take a few days off to celebrate that significant milestone anniversary, and Angel had gone on ahead to a farm the couple had recently purchased on the Mississippi River south of Angel's family home. Paul would have to finish the 10:00 p.m. Friday newscast and then, after a typically long day, drive through the night to join her.

Litchfield, Illinois, is a small town that lies on old Route 66 about fifty-five miles north of St. Louis. In 1950, this point on Paul's trip would have put him about five hours out of Chicago. In other words, it was probably close to 4:00 a.m. when the weary broadcaster dozed off behind the wheel of the car and woke up in a Springfield, Illinois, hospital.

The incident clearly spoiled the couple's anniversary getaway plans. Fortunately, Paul's injuries only required a hospital stay of a few days. Within a week, he was back on the air.

A more negative outcome would have done more than left Angel Harvey a widow with an infant son. It would have kept Paul from meeting a few months later the man who would be instrumental in launching him onto the national stage—WENR's landlord.

• • •

The Merchandise Mart, home to the radio studios in which Paul and Angel worked every day, was commissioned and built by department store giant Marshall Field & Co. in 1930. At the time of its completion, its twenty-five stories made it nowhere near the tallest building in the world or even on the block. But at over 4 million square feet of floor space, it was the *biggest* building on the planet. To this day, after almost eighty years of useful life, it remains within the top twenty-five of the world's largest commercial buildings.

It originally housed Marshall Field's wholesale showrooms and manufacturing facilities, plus the showrooms of retail tenants. The building allowed Marshall Field to centralize wholesale trade on a previously unheard-of scale. The site gave the company superior shipping and transport facilities and amenities including parking, restaurants, visitor lounges, a barbershop, and postal and telegraph offices. But by 1945, with the Great Depression and World War II having taken its toll on the retail world, Field's wholesale business had fallen off drastically.

Those desperate economic times forced many property owners to sell. However, some enormous fortunes were being made by men with cash who were buying. One of the most famous of these Depression-era tycoons was Joseph P. Kennedy, patriarch of the Kennedy political dynasty.

The Boston media and bootlegging mogul had purchased the Merchandise Mart in 1945 for the bargain price of $12.5 million. He had several of the lower floors renovated to accommodate office tenants of various types and visited the property from time to time to check up on his investment.

On one of these landlord visits around 1950, Kennedy was introduced to Paul Harvey. He was already acquainted with the thirty-two-year-old broadcaster's work. Kennedy had been listening to WENR on his visits to Chicago and liked both the style and the content of Paul's program. The staunchly anticommunist Bostonian particularly enjoyed Paul's pointed critiques of the Soviet Union and criticisms of those within the United States who passionately advocated turning America into a similar "socialist worker's paradise."

Kennedy came away from this chance meeting with the conviction that more people should be hearing this innovative conservative commentator. When he got back to Boston, he contacted the head of ABC Radio Networks in New York and told him he should elevate Paul to a spot on the nationwide network.

Whatever Joe Kennedy said, it was apparently persuasive. Of course, there is nothing so compelling as an idea whose time has come. Clearly, Paul Harvey's voice on radios across America was such an idea.

Before the lit ball in Times Square had dropped on New Year's Eve 1950, Paul found himself called up to the big leagues. And Angel found herself married to a network news commentator. Imagine that.

UN-AMERICAN ACTIVITIES

"How do you explain the intellectual witness? The fellow who's not a wild-eyed street corner rabble rouser . . . but is a sedate scientist with a whole string of degrees and yet who can calmly state to our lawmakers that yes he joined an organization which sought to overthrow the government of the United States . . . if necessary, by violence.

"We'd better learn to understand them. They are in our midst."

PAUL HARVEY
Autumn of Liberty (1954)

PAUL HARVEY PULLS HIS LONG OVERCOAT around him and buttons the top button as his two companions shiver in the cold beside his car. It is nearly 1:00 a.m. on February 6, 1951, and the temperature is below freezing and dropping rapidly.

The three had rendezvoused in Chicago at midnight as planned, ridden together in Paul's car about twenty-five miles southwest of the city on U.S. 66, and then pulled off the main road just before reaching the main turnoff for Lemont, Illinois. Then a series of turns on country and dirt farm roads led them into a grove of trees near a twelve-foot-high security fence with three strands of barbed wire at the top. Here, within the cover of the trees, Paul killed the headlights, pulled the car off the road, and shut it off. In the distance, beyond that security fence, the men could see the lights of Argonne National Laboratory, one of the most important and sensitive installations for top-secret atomic research in North America.

Now, fewer than sixty days after realizing his dream of becoming a national network news commentator, Paul is about to *become* national news, for within the hour he will be arrested and placed in federal custody on suspicion of espionage.

• • •

America's respite from war and the threat of war hadn't lasted very long. In many respects, it never came at all.

The ink was scarcely dry on the German surrender documents when General George Patton warned U.S. leaders and anyone else who would listen about the threat of Soviet expansionist ambitions. He had requested permission to use his Third Army to push the Russians out of Eastern Europe, where reports of atrocities and oppression by Stalin's forces were already leaking out. It was clear to everyone that the Soviets had no intention of relinquishing control of any of the blood-soaked territory they had covered on their push to Berlin. And the Soviet forces were in fact weak and vulnerable, having sustained losses of more than 10 million soldiers in the Eastern Front of the war and nearly as many civilian deaths.

General Dwight D. Eisenhower and newly installed president Harry Truman believed, probably correctly, that the war-weary American public had no stomach for a fight with a country that had been our ally only weeks earlier. Furthermore, there was still Japan to contend with.

A dizzying cascade of events seemed to validate Patton's warning over the next five years. In March of 1946 Winston Churchill stunned a still-celebrating America by declaring the demise of freedom across half an entire continent. In a speech titled "Sinews of Peace" at little Westminster College in Fulton, Missouri, Churchill had declared, "From Stettin in the Baltic to Trieste in the Adriatic, an iron curtain has descended across the Continent." That same year a Soviet-backed insurgency in Greece triggered a civil war in an effort to overthrow the pro-Western government in that country and install a communist dictatorship.

In 1948 the Soviet Union succeeded in installing a puppet government in Czechoslovakia and a few months later triggered a crisis with its blockade of Berlin. To the latter provocation, the West had been forced to respond with the Herculean and costly Berlin Airlift. The following year the most populous nation on earth became "Red" China as Mao Tse-tung's communist forces drove pro-Western Chinese president Chiang Kai-shek and his armies off the mainland to the island of Taiwan.

Almost simultaneously, the Soviet Union shocked the West when it successfully tested its first atomic bomb. American military and political leaders had assumed it would take the Soviets years, perhaps decades, to replicate the technological breakthroughs achieved by the United States through its supersecret Manhattan Project. The speed with which the Soviets had achieved nuclear parity caused many to suspect that American secrets were being leaked from within. Time would reveal that those suspicions were correct.

Communist Party of America members Julius and Ethel (Greenglass) Rosenberg, along with Ethel's brother David Greenglass, were instrumental in passing huge quantities of top secret U.S. military technology data to Soviet agents working inside America's borders. Not only were key secrets about the creation of atomic weapons passed along, the Rosenbergs had also delivered the complete plans for a "proximity fuse"—vital for the development of missile detonators—and a complete set of design and production drawings for the Lockheed P-80 Shooting Star jet fighter.

The Rosenbergs' betrayal of their country was uncovered in 1950, and they were tried and convicted the following year. They went to the electric chair in 1953 denying any involvement in espionage activity. Forty years later, however, when the collapse of the Soviet Union gave historians and reporters unprecedented access to

Kremlin archives, records from the time confirm that the Rosenbergs were indeed Soviet agents and had been instrumental in transferring nuclear bomb–making know-how to that country. Those records also reveal a labyrinth of other Soviet spying networks operating in the United States before, during, and after the two nations became allies during World War II. These networks reached into almost every sphere of American life—corporations, education, the arts, and even the federal government itself.

Some, like the Rosenberg ring, had been exposed. Most never were. As if all this weren't enough, there was one additional element about to be thrown into the stew of anxiety and mistrust simmering in the summer of 1950. In late June, communist North Korea, backed, armed, and aided by the Soviet Union, invaded South Korea. The invasion presented the United Nations, formed in the aftermath of World War II, with the first real test of its "collective security" doctrine and mandate. Led and prodded by Harry Truman, the United Nations intervened on behalf of South Korea. It was almost unbelievable. Less than four years after the bloody, global war to thwart the expansionist aims of the Nazis, America found itself sending young men into harm's way once more.

Though unreservedly anticommunist, Paul wasn't so sure this was America's war to fight. He was growing increasingly concerned about the security and strength of his own nation. Throughout 1945 and beyond, he had been among the voices in America urging suspicion of the Soviets and sounding warnings about clandestine Russian efforts to weaken and destabilize the world's only economic, military, and nuclear superpower. Indeed it was Paul's calm, reasoned eloquence in making the case for vigilance that had caught Joseph Kennedy's ear and led to the broadcaster's promotion to the network level.

Thus, when the Rosenberg spying case broke in the middle of 1950, it not only alarmed and dismayed Paul, it also confirmed some of his most visceral fears and suspicions. Countering these negative emotions was the exciting knowledge that his elevation to the network was scheduled to start in a few months. He and Angel were already in discussions with the ABC Radio Network's programming executives in New York about the what, when, and how of this new opportunity. It was an exhilarating time.

America received a unique gift on Christmas Day 1950. Anyone listening to an ABC Radio affiliate at noon that Monday, December 25, heard the words, "Hello, Americans, this is Paul Harvey. Stand by . . . for news!" The boy who "fell in love with words and ran away to join the radio" had been speaking into microphones since he was a gangly teenager in 1933. But he had never been able to say, "Hello, Americans" before. Hello, "Tulsans," yes. "Missoulans," indeed. And he had been greeting Chicagoans at night for six years. But this was the big leagues.

In addition to that trademark sign-on, any regular listener from the year 2000 would have heard much that was familiar were it possible to go back in time fifty years and hear that first nationwide broadcast. In the weeks leading up to this debut, Paul and Angel had settled on the straightforward name *Paul Harvey News and Comment* to identify the program. It remained the name of his primary newscast until the day he died. If he was going to be offering his opinions on the news—and that's precisely what he had been hired to do—he wanted that "Comment" sign hanging conspicuously on the storefront. He didn't have much use for journalists who feigned objectivity while selectively reporting only facts that fit their agendas.

Our time traveler would have heard "Page Two" and "Page Three" to identify the sponsorship commercial segments. And near the end of many of these network broadcasts, that same traveler would have heard a surprising or little-known item followed by the words, "And now you know . . . the *rest* of the story."

Many of the stories dominating the headlines in the opening

weeks of 1951 centered around what was coming to be known as the Cold War—a term coined by Democratic financier and presidential adviser Bernard Baruch. Each morning Paul's newspaper and the wire service tickers he pored over contained numerous items about Soviet spying, communist subversion in America, and testimony before the House Un-American Activities Committee (HUAC), testimony that grew more alarming with each passing week.

For example, on the morning of January 28, Paul would have opened his *Chicago Tribune* to find the following headline and article:

COLLEGE PROFS TELL WHY THEY BECAME REDS: SECRET TESTIMONY OF 2 RELEASED BY PROBERS Washington—Two college professors outlined the philosophy that led to their enlistment in the communist movement in secret testimony released today by the house un-American activities committee.

Prof. David Hawkins, 37, Texas-born, now professor of philosophy at the University of Colorado, who worked during the war on the ultra-secret atom bomb project at Los Alamos, N.M. . . .

Professor Kenneth O. May, 35, Oregon-born, now associate professor of mathematics at Carleton college, Northfield, Minn., who lost his teaching position at the University of Berkeley, in 1940 because of communist activities.[1]

Even before moving his broadcast over to the network, Paul had made lax security measures at many of the nation's sensitive research facilities a regular focus of his commentaries. There had been too many reports of breaches and compromises at civilian and university-run facilities that were doing important work for the military. When reporting one of these incidents, Paul would ask, "When are we going to start taking seriously the protecting of these secrets that are keys to our competitive advantage in the arms race and perhaps the keys to our very survival?"

One of the most important keepers of such secrets was in Paul's backyard—Argonne National Laboratory (ANL). ANL refers to itself as "America's first national laboratory," and with good reason. Established during World War II as the Manhattan Engineering District's Metallurgical Laboratory operated by the University of Chicago, it was officially renamed Argonne National Laboratory in 1946. The lab boasted having some of the top scientific minds in the country and was a key part of the Manhattan Project team that successfully developed the first atomic bomb.

By 1950, ANL was not only one of the U.S. Department of Energy's oldest research and engineering labs, it was the largest. Some of the most important and sensitive research being done there involved the creation of small, manageable nuclear reactors, the kind that would ultimately enable the creation of nuclear submarines. But Argonne did not have a spotless record where security was concerned.

On February 8, 1949, Argonne gained unwanted attention when a bottle containing thirty-one grams of enriched uranium went missing from one of the lab's vaults. An investigation ultimately found that about twenty-four grams of the material had been shipped to Oak Ridge National Laboratory in Tennessee. The balance of the material was eventually found in Argonne's landfill. The congressional investigation that followed resulted in a review and reworking of Argonne's tracking procedures of such materials.

Sometime in late 1950 or very early 1951, amid this steady stream of reports about spying and subversion around the nation, Paul received a call from Fred Busbey, a U.S. congressman from Illinois and a personal friend of his. Representative Busbey had someone he thought Paul would be interested in talking to. He couldn't elaborate over the phone. Paul was intrigued and agreed to meet the man.

The mystery man turned out to be Charles Rogal, a part-time security guard and switchboard operator at ANL. He told the broadcaster a story of sloppy security, poorly followed protocols, and underqualified security staff. To Paul, it sounded like another deeply damaging espionage loss to the Soviets just waiting to happen.

Paul formulated a plan. Whether it was a foolhardy scheme or not has been debated for five decades. Nevertheless, Paul contacted a man he knew who worked for the Office of Naval Intelligence, John Crowley, and persuaded him to join him and Charles Rogal on that trip out to the security fence in those early morning hours of February 6, 1951.

• • •

As his two companions watched, Paul began to scale the fence. When he reached the top, however, his overcoat snagged on the barbed wire. He struggled for several minutes to pull free, and before he could get clear, a jeep patrolling the perimeter happened by.

When his companions saw the headlights approaching, they slipped off behind some bushes and then ran off through the trees. They eventually came to the main road and caught a ride back to town. Unfortunately for them, they left a wallet and some identifying papers behind in the car.

The following day, puzzled *Tribune* readers learned of this improbable event:

PAUL HARVEY SEIZED INSIDE ATOM LAB AREA

Paul H. Aurandt, 3400 Lake Shore Dr., an American Broadcasting Company radio and television newscaster under the name of Paul Harvey, was seized by a guard at the Argonne National Laboratory in DuPage county at 1:10 a.m. yesterday, a few minutes after he had climbed a fence surrounding the laboratory's restricted area.

News of the arrest was released in a statement by the atomic energy commission only after it was approved "at the highest level" in Washington. Aurandt was turned over to Federal Bureau of Investigation agents for questioning and later released.

Later in the day Aurandt said: "I have been working in conjunction and cooperation with the investigating divisions of several departments of the United States government for the last several months. I am not at liberty nor am I authorized by the governmental investigating divisions to release any story or information concerning the matters upon which I have been working."[2]

Follow-up stories appeared in papers across the country for several days thereafter, with much speculation about what government agencies, if any, Paul may have been working with to test ANL's security measures. Few in the general public or the press seemed inclined to believe that Paul Harvey was a Soviet spy. Federal investigators, on the other hand, weren't so sure. Records indicate they didn't know *what* to make of the incident.

Everyone had an opinion about it, though. University of Chicago professor and researcher Dr. Harold Urey, winner of the 1934 Nobel Prize in chemistry, was quoted as saying he was disappointed that guards did not shoot Harvey. When reporters asked accomplice Charles Rogal—who was fired by Argonne after the incident—if there had been any fear of being shot by guards, he said, "Not one of them could shoot and hit the side of a barn."[3]

There was much mirth and joking surrounding the whole thing, but it didn't change the fact that Paul was potentially in serious trouble. The federal government was planning to bring charges that carried a possible ten-year prison term and $10,000 in fines.

A federal grand jury was called. Presiding was a future Illinois governor, U.S. attorney Otto Kerner. He heard the charges against Paul: "conspiracy to obtain information on national security and transmit it to the public."[4] In response, the broadcaster requested permission from Kerner to appear before the grand jury. Kerner agreed on one condition: Paul had to first sign a waiver of the right to later claim immunity from prosecution for anything his testimony might reveal.

The accused happily signed it. The professional talker apparently had a high degree of confidence that if he could get the ear of the grand jury, they would view his act as more of a public service than a crime. His appearance was scheduled for March 21.

In the interim, the feds' view of Paul apparently softened considerably. The Chicago office of the FBI even filed a supplemental report, indicating that, upon further study, the Justice Department had reached the conclusion "that Aurandt had not willfully violated security laws." Paul also received a good word from an unexpected source. As the *Tribune* reported, "Merlin W. Griffith, business agent of the Argonne security guards union, yesterday praised Aurandt for exposing what Griffith charged were security 'flaws' at Argonne."[5]

Paul's confidence turned out to be well-founded, and his appearance must have had its desired effect. On April 4, 1951, the grand jury voted not to indict him. Later the foreman of the grand jury told the press the vote was not even close.

• • •

Precisely what Paul was thinking when he climbed the fence that night remains a matter of debate. It was something that, in his later years, he declined to talk about. It seems most improbable that he was working officially on behalf of any government agency. If a high-level department wanted to see if Argonne's perimeter could be breached, they would almost certainly *not* recruit a radio newsman in a wool overcoat for the task.

Perhaps a savvy self-marketer who had just gotten himself a national newscast thought it would be a brilliant promotional ploy to breach one of the country's most sensitive facilities. The headlines would really put him on the map. But this motivation seems deeply out of character with everything else we know about the life and values of Paul Harvey. The most plausible explanation is the most obvious one.

What he learned from Charles Rogal about the security situation at Argonne must have troubled him profoundly. In the wake of the ongoing Rosenberg affair, he was concerned that secrets and technologies vital to the safety and survival of our nation were at risk. He and others had been publicly calling for greater vigilance for several years but without apparent effect. So he took it upon himself to expose the vulnerability the only way he knew how.

It would be like a volunteer fireman setting a small blaze to create a firebreak, in hopes of keeping an inferno from destroying his town. The fact that this would-be firefighter could easily have gotten himself shot either didn't occur to him or didn't matter.

What was clear to Paul in early 1951 was that communism was spreading like a prairie fire in a drought all over the world and that inexplicably—maddeningly—a good number of the brightest, most talented, and most privileged of his fellow Americans considered this a good thing. Even more bewildering to him was the desire of some of them to bring that fire to our shores.

So for a time, Paul would cheer the work being done on Capitol Hill by the House Un-American Activities Committee. That Congress was working to set firebreaks at the federal level seemed an eminently sensible and praiseworthy thing. But as he would discover before the decade had run its course, sometimes the flames of a firebreak can blaze out of control.

CHAPTER 7

COLD WAR, HOT EMOTIONS

"The communism which is corrupting Americans today is not a movement inspired by the poor, but by the cowardly pseudo-intellectual rich. [They] suffer from the guilt complex of those to whom success came too cheaply."

PAUL HARVEY
Remember These Things (1952)

A BITING JANUARY WIND slices through the rail yard of Chicago's Union Station as the Milwaukee-Pacific Railroad's *Olympian Hiawatha* diesel out of St. Paul hisses to a halt. Trackside, a large group of photographers and reporters, once huddled for warmth and conversation, now jockey for position in anticipation of the arrival of the most sought-after interview in the country.

The door of the first-class car opens and out steps a beaming Paul Harvey, wearing a long wool overcoat, neck scarf, and Stetson fedora. Given their reaction, this is not the face the reporters hoped to see. "What are you doing on that train, Harvey?" one reporter shouts.

"Just coming home, fellows. Gave a speech in Aberdeen last night."

"Did you see Mrs. Llewellyn in there?" another asks. "Did you talk to her?"

The broadcaster doesn't answer. He just gives the group a smile reminiscent of a satisfied feline sitting next to the open, empty canary cage.

The official representative from Chicago's NBC-TV affiliate groans and swears under his breath.

"Paul, you have to be the luckiest so-and-so I know," a photographer says.

"I don't believe in luck, Mike," Paul says, his smile becoming less playful. "I'm a praying man and that's always been all I need to be in the right place at the right time. Gotta go!" Paul turns on his heel and heads through the beautiful beaux arts terminal.

• • •

On January 23, 1955, being in the right place at the right time allowed Paul to scoop NBC's *Today Show* and the rest of the national press on a story that had captured the entire country's attention. It was a sensational news event that had been two years in the making.

An American B-29 bomber with her crew of fourteen had been dropping leaflets over North Korea on January 12, 1953, when it vanished. It was presumed shot down. The Korean War had been raging for two and a half years, but now peace talks were progressing and it seemed a negotiated truce might be achieved soon. The leaflets were messages to the North Korean people announcing that the South Koreans, and the UN forces that had come to their aid, wanted peace. Seven months later, an armistice was, in fact, signed.

When prisoners of war and remains of the fallen were exchanged shortly thereafter, there was no sign of the missing B-29's crew. Indeed, a number of other missing-in-action pilots and crew remained unaccounted for after the war as well. Their families presumed they were dead, but as is the case with many loved ones of MIAs, there was always a haunting sense of uncertainty and occasional wisps of hope.

Then, more than a year after the end of the war, news suddenly emerged that seventeen U.S. soldiers were alive and being held prisoner—in communist China! Seventeen American families had gotten loved ones back as though from the dead. The story captivated the imagination of the entire nation.

Before long the Chinese government announced that it was putting thirteen of the men on trial for espionage. One of the captive men was Captain Elmer Fred Llewellyn of Missoula, Montana. Over the course of the next few months, the men were tried and sentenced to various prison terms in China. Meanwhile the United States, in conjunction with the United Nations, worked to secure their release and return to America.

In January 1955, China made another surprise move. Seeking to exploit the men for propaganda purposes, as well as to use them as bargaining chips to gain UN membership, the Chinese suddenly invited the families of the men to come to China and visit their loved ones.

The U.S. State Department discouraged the families from taking the trip, saying they couldn't guarantee their safety. However, the wives announced that they desperately wanted to visit their husbands but that the costs were prohibitive. One of them was Mrs. Marjorie Llewellyn—wife of Captain Fred Llewellyn. Hearing of their plight, a Kansas City businessman stepped forward and offered to pay the women's expenses.

On January 23, Mrs. Llewellyn and her mother-in-law boarded a train in Missoula and headed for Chicago. She and her husband's mother were traveling at the invitation and at the expense of NBC's *Today Show*, with which she had agreed to do an interview about their upcoming trip. The show's producers were thrilled that their program would be the first major news outlet to bring Mrs. Llewellyn's thoughts and feelings to the fascinated country. Thus, the *Today Show* reporter was dismayed to see Paul step off of Mrs. Llewellyn's train.

Paul had indeed just happened to be on the train. Of course, he recognized the freshly minted celebrity, and having formerly worked at a Missoula radio station, found much to chat about with the two ladies.

The next morning, it was Paul who broke the news of the women's upcoming trip and of their generous benefactor.

• • •

Paul had been thrilled to have a good news story to report about the aftermath of the Korean conflict. Throughout the war he had been a consistent critic of the entire operation, though always expressing the utmost admiration for the valor and devotion of the men of the U.S. armed forces. His reasons for being critical of the war were many and heartfelt.

First among these was the refusal by the U.S. government and the UN to call the conflict a war. It was a "police action," officials in Washington insisted. Right behind this objection was the fact that this "police action" was a UN-run operation. American soldiers were being asked to march under—and die under—the light blue UN flag, and that didn't sit well with the patriotic broadcaster.

In his 1952 book, *Remember These Things*, Paul doesn't pull any punches in explaining his feelings about the conflict:

> We are told that what is happening in Korea is not really a war.
>   But a lot of American boys are just as dead as if it were.
>   I am going to call it what it is: a bloody, rotten, thankless war.[1]

This kind of language might surprise people who only know Paul Harvey from what they've been told rather than from what the man actually said and wrote throughout his life. In truth, he was much more complicated than the warmongering caricature drawn by his detractors on the Left. Combined with his passionate love of country and reverence for the service and sacrifice of soldiers was the heart of a pacifist handed down from his Anabaptist forebearers, and the instincts of an isolationist going back to his heroes William Allen White and Charles Lindbergh.

Yes, he despised communism and recognized Red China and the Soviet Union as grave threats to the survival of the United States. But he perceived our most plausible threat was not that America would be overrun by bayonet-carrying enemies from without; it was that a drowsy, comfortable America would gradually succumb to creeping socialism and crumble from within.

Again, from *Remember These Things*:

> Maybe to a few, Korea is what they say it is. A challenge intended to stop Soviet Russia.
>
> Maybe they really believe we have got to contain communism where it is, or be consumed by it. If they do, if this is their studied view, then I say it is high time they carried out the plan and get it over with.[2]

That final statement goes to the heart of Paul's problem with America's involvement in Korea. The cost in lives was horrendous. As he points out in his book, in the three years of war against Japan in the huge Pacific Theater, America lost twenty thousand men. But American losses in tiny Korea, "fighting with weapons and tactics prescribed by the United Nations," equaled this number in less than half the time. Before the war ended, America's killed in action exceeded 36,000. The next allied nation involved, Great Britain, lost only 1,109 men. Australia, 339. Paul wondered why a UN flag was flying when Americans were doing all the dying.

The Paul Harvey of 1952—and of 1962, for that matter—believed that if victory over communists in a small Asian nation was important enough to warrant the sacrifice of tens of thousands of American boys, then it warranted using any and all of the weapons and tactics at our disposal—especially if using them would save many of those soldiers' lives. And he meant *any* and *all*:

> I vote that we make this phony war a real one and I recommend, on the basis of General MacArthur's proposal, that our first battle maneuver be to silence our little guns and stop killing Chinese and stop killing Americans and get out our big guns and get this thing over with.[3]

Of course, we all tend to soften our positions as we grow older. Who among us holds precisely the same views at fifty-five that we did at twenty-five? But in hearing the Paul Harvey of the early Cold War era, it is clear that he viewed America's tendency to try to play a global chess game with the Soviets—rushing aid and advisers and armies to various points around the globe to counter perceived communist inroads and incursions—as an insidious trap. It's easy to forget that the early international anticommunist crusaders were mostly Democrats—Truman, JFK, LBJ—whereas Paul was an old-school Republican of the isolationist stripe.

He viewed Washington's obsession with trying to stymie the Soviets all over the planet as a dangerous distraction we could not afford. He called it "forcing guns and funds on reluctant friends . . . because we are afraid."[4] A distraction from what, you ask.

He saw it as a distraction from confronting the two *real* threats to America's prosperity and freedom. In Paul's view, the first threat was among us. The second was within each of us.

• • •

"He supported McCarthy in the 1950s."

This line in varying forms appeared in virtually every obituary and biographical sketch of Paul Harvey after his death on the last day of February 2009. In even the most respectful of profiles, the detail was meant to show that he wasn't perfect, that there was at least one negative item to set alongside that long list of extraordinary achievements and admirable attributes.

Those who didn't care for Harvey's conservative philosophy and traditional moral values were less tactful. "He had a face for radio and the political compass of the Inquisition," insisted one popular blogger.[5] Other ungracious send-offs contained the words *McCarthyite*, *witch hunt*, and the *Red Scare*. Even *Time* magazine joined the fray, with correspondent Richard Corliss writing, "The rosy sentimentalist was also a fretful conservative; he backed Joe McCarthy's search for imaginary communists in the State Department."[6]

Yet what is astonishing about such allegations is not their vehemence but the historical ignorance of those who made them. The truth is that much of what Paul Harvey suspected in the 1950s was true: communists had infiltrated the American government, the Communist Party in the United States was a servant of their masters in Moscow, and more than a few senior U.S. officials were fellow travelers in the communist cause. These assertions are not witchhunting or red-baiting or the delusions of a hard-drinking senator from Wisconsin. No, these assertions are now historical fact.

In the years after the breakup of the Soviet empire in 1989, Boris Yeltsin threw open the Communist Party's records, including the huge archive of the Communist International, or Comintern. This agency had overseen the many foreign Communist parties in the first part of the twentieth century. Sometime later, in 1994, the Russian SVR—which had replaced the KGB—also opened its archives to researchers who could pay for the privilege in order to help fill the SVR's badly diminished coffers. Then, in an equally surprising move, in 1995 the U.S. government released thousands of KGB cables that had been intercepted and decoded in the 1940s via a top secret operation called VENONA. From these sources, more than 2 million pages of new documents on Soviet activity suddenly became available to researchers.

This avalanche of information confirmed, among many other important truths, that Paul Harvey had been right. The Communist Party of America was a tool of the Soviet Union and not an independent agency, as its members had claimed. As one journalist has summarized, "The CPUSA was founded in Moscow, funded from Moscow . . . and directed by Moscow."[7] The documents also reveal that the spy networks within our government were much more extensive than even the most wild-eyed alarmist of the 1950s ever suggested. The same journalist summarized the new findings: "Hundreds of CPUSA members had infiltrated the American government and were passing information to the KGB. They honeycombed the State Department and the Office of Strategic Services. Virtually all of the revisionists' martyrs really were spilling secrets to the Kremlin, including Alger Hiss, the Rosenbergs, and a pair of Roosevelt aides, Harry Dexter White and Laurence Duggan."[8]

These revelations were confirmation of Paul Harvey's worst fears. And they raised some nerve-racking possibilities. For example, if Franklin Roosevelt had died in his third term, rather than early in his fourth, his vice president, Henry Wallace, would have become president. Yet Wallace was on record as saying if he were president he would appoint the above-mentioned Harry Dexter White to be secretary of the treasury and would name Laurence Duggan secretary of state. Chillingly, the VENONA cables reveal beyond any doubt that both men were Soviet spies.

Despite such overwhelming evidence, the prevailing myths were not easily uprooted. For too long, movies and college textbooks and confident elites had told the American people that Joseph McCarthy was a fool, that the Red Scare was not unlike the witch trials of seventeenth-century Salem, and that there was, in truth, little to fear from a communist threat. Though the facts of history, and even the archives of the Soviets themselves showed otherwise, such revisionism would live on and even rear its head in the obituaries written at Paul Harvey's death. Thankfully, we know now what Americans should have known then: men like Paul Harvey were not only patriots; they were right about communist enemies both without and within.

Yet these beliefs did not make Paul a rabid follower of Joseph McCarthy. In fact, by 1950, when McCarthy began drawing national attention, much of the hard work of exposing communists and raising awareness had already been done by numerous public figures and by the famous House Un-American Activities Committee. Though Paul celebrated the work of this committee, he grew suspicious of McCarthy and his demagoguery. Contrary to the accepted wisdom, he was ambivalent about McCarthy almost from the beginning. "I was not a fan of Joe McCarthy . . . but of McCarthyism,"[9] he would say later—meaning he had supported efforts in Congress to identify and root out Soviet spy networks in our nation.

By 1954, however, it was clear to Paul that all the attention had gone to McCarthy's head, that the senior member of the Senate Committee on Government Operations was getting carried away, and that his grandstanding and scaremongering was actually counterproductive to Paul's hopes for smaller, more limited government in the post-FDR era. He clearly had Joe McCarthy in mind when he wrote:

> The brief-case warriors took to the microphones, warned of "terrible dangers," "Communist perils." Day after day the grim reminders of atom bombs and hundreds of Red divisions.
>
> Fear spreads, confusion spreads, spending spurts higher . . . higher than man's imagination.[10]

By 1955, Paul believed the most fundamental threat to America's continued strong existence was twofold. First, there were many in our midst who wanted to take America down the road of big-government socialism and who promised security, "equality," and comfort before the masses to sell the deal. The second threat was that prosperity was making Americans soft, complacent, and greedy, and therefore susceptible to the allure of government dependency.

In other words, the first threat was the presence of siren song singers in our midst. The second was our universal attraction to such songs.

A deeply moral man, Paul saw our internal vulnerability as a moral problem:

> If the old pioneering fire has died out of us, if we will hang onto new deals, fair deals and raw deals at the sacrifice of our I-deals, then we deserve to be trapped by our own clutching fingers because we are animals, nothing more.
>
> History, for six-thousand years, is the record of free people made slaves trying to get the free lunch out of the bottle.[11]

The complex truth about Paul Harvey is that he did encourage and praise the efforts to expose communist spies in the 1940s and early 1950s and that recent scholarship has vindicated his concerns. It is equally true that when Joe McCarthy started making accusations he couldn't support, tarring people with too broad and indiscriminate a brush, and threatening the liberties Paul cherished, he withdrew his support.

Though Paul had to battle to keep his fundamental optimism alive when he viewed the state of his nation, on a personal level, the 1950s were very good to him and Angel. The jump to the ABC network made him a rising national star. The couple's income grew, demand for Paul as a public speaker soared, and his schedule filled.

Still, they found time on as many weekends as possible to slip down to Reveille Ranch—the Mississippi River farm in Missouri that was quickly becoming Paul's place to reconnect with the mind and heart of rural America. In a newspaper column that he wrote from the farm in 1951, Paul gives us a glimpse into how important these country connections were to him.

The piece is as revealing as it is beautifully written:

Nothing earth-shaking is happening out at the ranch. Small Paul is pacing the floor outside the hen-house door. Baby ducks are due any time now.

The apples are ripening round and red.

The birds are awake while the morning is still asleep so the sun can come up to music.

As I said . . . nothing earth-shaking. Just a little loafing and a lot of living and a miracle every seven minutes.

Maybe I could see more clearly now because there was less hair in my eyes.

Or maybe it's because my library was mostly back in Chicago and I went right to the hill folks for my answers.

They are not asking anything for nothing. They'll grow their own meat and potatoes and make their own gravy. But they have one bad habit . . . they just will not lock their doors.

To us, for whom life is half done, it will not matter much.

But one day may others belong to these green acres . . . because we deserved them . . . because we fought all enemies to preserve them . . . all enemies . . . foreign and DOMESTIC.

Lock the door. Oil the shotgun over the mantel. And stay aware!

For the new enemies of American freedom pose as friends bearing gifts.

Now, my learned contemporaries of high degree . . . I am aware that my recommendations for hanging onto your Republic with both hands circumvent most of your geo-political considerations.

You speak for the architects . . . I'll speak for the builders . . .

the men who can straighten rusty nails and build this all over again.

Here in the hills and plains are the builders . . . wherever their towers rise.

And to know them is to understand why God so often chose the simple ones . . . to confound the wise.[12]

CHAPTER 8

A SNAPSHOT
IN HISTORY

*"I don't think of myself as a profound journalist. I think of myself
as a professional parade watcher who can't wait to get out of bed
every morning and rush down to the Teletypes and pan for gold."*

PAUL HARVEY

PAUL HARVEY IS IN SAVANNAH, GEORGIA, for a speaking engage-
ment. It is November 18, 1963. As is his practice when away from
his Chicago base, he relies on the kindness of the ABC radio affiliates.
On this day he will borrow the studios of WSGA to record his five-
minute 9:00 a.m. news summary and the fifteen-minute newscast
at noon—both heard on ABC stations around the country and on
Armed Forces Radio all over the world.

On this day, President John F. Kennedy, son of the man who
played a key role in giving Paul this national platform, is down the
road a bit from Savannah visiting Tampa, Florida. The president will
head back to Washington this day so that he and the First Lady can
prepare for a two-day, five-city tour of Texas, including a stop in
Dallas on November 22—a stop, as we now know, that will be the
last of his presidency.

Here—at a point in Paul's career at which he has had almost thirty
years of experience communicating by microphone and has been a

national voice for well over a decade—he is at the top of his game. He is a vigorous forty-five-year-old with everything that made him remarkable and memorable and significant fully on display.

No description of this artist's life or analysis of his work would be complete without taking one of his masterful fifteen-minute newscasts and giving it a thorough dissection. A close inspection of a single broadcast can be wonderfully enlightening. In it we can find much more than insight into the man's style and methods. In it we'll find truth about his worldview—his "breed" of American and his heart.

As important, the news items he will handle rapidly but with a poet's grace on this day touch virtually all of what will become the searing national issues of the second half of the twentieth century: the Cold War, the Middle East, Vietnam, the civil rights movement, the political realignment of the South, Cuba, the space race, and rapid technological change each make their appearance here. All this in a fifteen-minute newscast and with time allowed for some humor, whimsy, and quirkiness to lighten the air and balance the relentlessly negative. Add to this Paul's trademark timing and dramatization, and it's almost a piece of performance art.

Before we explore this classic Paul Harvey method, a brief note about the format of these excerpts. Usually when quoting someone, the use of ellipses (. . .) indicates that some material has been omitted. In the quotations below, however, ellipses are used to indicate those pregnant pauses in delivery that so characterized Paul Harvey's style. You will also see some words in all capital letters to indicate points he inflected heavily for emphasis. The hope is that you will better "hear" his familiar voice when you read the words.

Now, let's wade into this edition of *Paul Harvey News and Comment* and, as he would say, pan for gold:

Hello, Americans. This is Paul Harvey. Stand by . . . for news!

Naturally. The man learned early in his career the power of audible branding. It didn't matter whether you were listening to the Paul Harvey of the 1960s, 1970s, 1980s, 1990s, or the new millennium; not only were the words of the greeting the same, the inflection was always identical—though the timbre of the voice began to quaver a bit in that final decade.

He opens this newscast with what will be the dominant headline in most papers that morning, a big fire in Atlantic City:

> . . . *more than two score persons dead, or presumed dead, and all of them were guests at The Surfside. A hotel . . . for elderly persons.*

Here Paul condenses a long, complex story into a few sentences and points us, without elaboration or exploitation, to the one detail of the story that we would most care about. He moves on to quickly touch on a big sports story:

> *In the sportlight . . . Detroit's Tigers sure enough did it . . . traded slugger Rocky Colavito to Kansas City . . . traded Colavito and pitcher Bob Anderson, and MONEY, for three . . . Jerry Lumpe, Ed Rakow, and Dave Wickersham.*

By the way, this is the Rocky Colavito who three years earlier had been traded to the Tigers by the Cleveland Indians—bringing down upon the heads of the Indians (at least in the minds of their long-suffering fans) "the curse of Rocky Colavito." The earlier trade initiated a thirty-three-year drought in which the Indians never finished higher than eleven games out of first place in their division.

Paul moves on to note the retirement of Georgia Congressman Carl Vinson at age eighty:

For all of my life he's been a fixture . . . for almost fifty years, this distinguished Georgia Democrat has been one of THE most powerful voices in the Senate for fiscal responsibility and military preparedness. His health appears fine, but Senator Vinson has had eighty birthdays, including today's, and he wants the rest of his years free from official responsibility.

Though it contains a rare mistake as he talks about the congressman's work in the "Senate," this mention of Representative Vinson brings us to a key characteristic of that moment in history and of Paul Harvey's well-thought-out value system. Vinson had become a congressman in 1914, and, as Paul Harvey reports above, retired after fifty years in the House. Throughout that time, Vinson had been a champion for national defense and especially the U.S. Navy and the Marine Corps. In fact, a nuclear-powered aircraft carrier was named for him, the USS *Carl Vinson*, making him one of a handful of living Americans to have a navy vessel carry his name. On March 15, 1980, at age ninety-six, Vinson attended the ship's launching. This record, as well as a legislative approach guided by a belief that a federal government governs best that governs least, earned Vinson great appreciation and respect from Paul.

At the same time, Vinson, like most Southern Democrats of his era in Congress, was a segregationist. In 1956 he had joined one hundred other Southern politicians (ninety-nine Democrats and two Republicans) in signing The Southern Manifesto—a response to the Supreme Court's landmark *Brown v. Board of Education* decision of 1954, which had declared racially segregated schools unconstitutional.

In November 1963, the civil rights movement in America was just getting a full head of steam, although President Kennedy, while verbally supportive, was not nearly the White House ally of civil rights leaders that Lyndon Johnson would ultimately become in the months ahead. In this moment, it is still possible for a Christian man of conscience like Paul to praise Carl Vinson for the important things about which he'd been right for the last fifty years and simply be silent about one big thing on which Vinson had been wrong.

And as we'll see before this newscast concludes, Paul himself is in the midst of his own struggle to reconcile the conflicting pulls of some of his most deeply held principles regarding liberty and freedom of opportunity in the face of clear injustice.

The first segment of the newscast continues:

Glenda Underiner, secretary, twenty-six. Moved from St. Louis, Missouri, to New York City six weeks ago. Last night, she sat in front of her mirror, tiring her hair in her furnished room in Queens, and suddenly slumped over dead from a sniper's bullet through the window. The window through which the bullet came faces the Long Island Railroad tracks.

You can tell a great deal about journalists or editors simply by observing which stories they choose to report and which ones they ignore. Paul is no exception, and he chooses this story, among the scores he could have reported, for a reason. First, it probably passes the "Betty" test with flying colors. You'll recall that he ran every potential item through the filter of this question: "Would my sister-in-law, Betty, on her farm in the Midwest, care about this story?"

In this case—a young girl leaving provincial St. Louis for the bright lights of New York City, only to be killed in a bizarre homicide after a mere six weeks—well, that sounds like something Betty and the gals would be discussing with sadness and wonder down at the beauty parlor that afternoon. But the story also harmonizes with a fundamental pillar of Paul's worldview. Namely, that not much good happens out in places like New York City or Los Angeles. That the glitter and newness and bustle are not only illusive but also danger-ous. It is telling that he repeatedly refused throughout his professional life to relocate to New York City. Of course, as we've already seen, there were other reasons. As he told an interviewer in 1973:

> If there is an ill in broadcast journalism, it's not out in the grass roots. It's on Manhattan Island. And that's purely a geographical phenomenon. Our press and information centers, our news networks, our major news magazines, are all epicentered in New York City. If the rest of the country gets a distorted perspective down the line, it results not from some sinister international conspiracy, not from lack of conscientiousness, but merely from the fact that the hub of the wheel is that far off center.[1]

By the way, the term *tiring* to refer to a woman's evening brushing of her hair is a term from a much older time. Wasn't the recommended goal for women one hundred strokes? It seems Paul was a living anachronism even back in 1963. His newscast rolls on:

> *Yale's professor Barghoorn back home in Connecticut says he was NOT spying in Russia, that there was NO justification for his arrest and detention, says he was interrogated . . . incessantly. At the same time, eleven Soviet scientists are today on an inspection tour . . . of our national atomic laboratory . . . in Oak Ridge, Tennessee. (Long pause to let that sink in.)*

Here we have the genius of Paul Harvey's nuanced brand of commentary on display. Keep in mind that this is the man who spent much of the 1940s and 1950s warning about the duplicity of the Soviets and decrying lax security in our sensitive research installations. Yet all he does here is gently lay the two following one-line stories side by side for our inspection and then step back. He doesn't rail. He doesn't preach. He doesn't even connect the dots for us. He thinks enough of our common sense to let us do that for ourselves:

Item 1: Soviets needlessly interrogate a visiting American professor for two weeks because they're paranoid and hypervigilant about *their* secrets.

Item 2: We're throwing open the door to Soviet scientists, some of whom are most certainly KGB agents, because we're careless with ours.

By simply placing these two items side by side before us, he invites us to make of the comparison what we will—to find irony or lunacy or nothing at all. But by listening oh, so very closely in that long pause following the final word, you can almost hear the newscaster wearily shaking his head.

Then the tone and volume change abruptly:

Havana. Ouch! Communism hurts! They didn't tell us it was going to be like this. When Fidel Castro was leading his rebels down from the hills, he told them they were fighting Batista, and the United Fruit Company, and the imperialists of the United States. He promised all these things the rich people had, we the workers one day will have. But he forgot to tell them they'd have to keep working.

He neglected to explain that the rich people got rich the only way there is to get rich—by working. And this puts a different complexion on the revolution. The leisure-loving Latin who loves to sit in the shade or play in the surf saw the rich people languishing on the Varadero beaches and dreamed that this would be his life after the revolution.

But now? . . . Well, Cuba is desperately hungry, a universally needy nation. . . . They took it away from the rich people all right. So now everybody is poor.

And today the brutal taskmaster of the revolutionary government, Minister of Industry Che Guevara, decrees longer hours with less pay in the cane fields. And no malingering.

> *Over Havana radio Guevara says Cuba's principal difficulty is the lack of desire of the people to work. . . . So from now on he says any work stoppage will be construed as antirevolutionary . . . and any striker will be shot. . . . It's a rude awakening for the Cuban peasant. His work is harder. His reward is less than before. But perhaps worst of all . . . his dream is gone.*

The details of this news report would likely come as a shock to today's legions of trendy young Che Guevara T-shirt wearers. Che has been reinvented as a romantic freedom fighter. The truth, however, is much less glamorous. Or liberal, for that matter.

Che was an Argentine revolutionary who played the role of Castro's enforcer. As such, he presided over hundreds of executions. Many of these he performed personally. He said he enjoyed it. The man whose poster has adorned countless campus dorm rooms also established Cuba's labor-camp system in which thousands of dissidents, artists, pastors, and democracy advocates suffered and died.

Of course, Paul didn't choose and write this story as a rebuttal to American academics and artists who were tempted to romanticize a despot—and there were plenty of them.

Instead, he wanted his listeners to hear this story as a reminder to guard against the siren song of socialism here at home. In fact, *siren song* is precisely the metaphor Paul uses in the opening section of his 1954 antisocialist book of warning, titled *Autumn of Liberty*. Calling for a revival of self-reliance and personal responsibility, he writes:

> There is no easy success.
> No free lunch.
> No guaranteed rocking chair.
> We must drown out the siren's song which leads men to expect these things . . . drown out the strange music . . . by letting freedom ring![2]

No, he chose this story because he simply wanted the disillusion-ment and misery of the poor, duped Cubans to serve as a cautionary tale to us. He wasn't for overthrowing Castro nearly as much as he was for keeping American versions of Castro from overthrowing us.

Paul's newscast this day then turns to three quick stories in succes-sion. He mentions discussions of whom the Republicans are thinking about running for president against the incumbent JFK in 1964. He mentions the odds-on favorite, Barry Goldwater, but also points out that "GOP Congressional Committee Chairman Bob Wilson thinks Senator Margaret Chase Smith deserves a crack at the job. Says he thinks she has great possibilities." Smith was the long-serving Republican senator from Maine.

He then mentions a story about limits being placed on the dis-tances active-duty servicemen can travel while on furlough. It seems they've been trying to cover too much distance on a three-day pass and end up driving too fast to get back. And he brings us an amazing story of a man who bought a two-dollar book of stamps at a New York post office, noticed they had some printing imperfections, and ended up selling them for ten thousand dollars.

Then he offers one of those classic Paul Harvey moments that ends up in *Reader's Digest* and is tacked to office bulletin boards all over the country. It captures the heart of why Paul thought radio was a superior medium to television's moving pictures:

Today you and I are visiting in the studios of WSGA in Savannah, Georgia, and over the desk which I have borrowed for this day is a message I read on an earlier visit today, but in case you missed it, I want you to hear it. It says, and hear this closely now:

"You say one picture is worth a thousand words? Well, let's see about that.

"You give me one thousand words and I'll give you the

Lord's Prayer AND the 23rd Psalm; and the Hippocratic Oath; and a sonnet by Shakespeare; and the Preamble to the Constitution; and Lincoln's Gettysburg Address; and I'll still have enough words left over for just about all of the Boy Scout oath.

"And I wouldn't trade you those things for any picture on earth."

It's easy to guess why Paul was so taken with this little tribute to the power of words that he reads it on both broadcasts this day. He loved them. In a speech he once said, "Trust me to paint pictures on the mirror of your mind and I will let you feel such agony and ecstasy, such misery and majesty . . . as you would never be able to feel by merely looking at it."[3]

Then we hear the famous words, "Page Two," followed by a heart-felt word or two on behalf of the good folks at Bankers Life and Casualty. Then we hear something quite remarkable.

What follows will be by far the longest item of any he brings us today. It is not news. But on its face, it is not quite pure commentary as we usually think of it. It is an audio essay that is a masterpiece of subtlety and nuance. So subtle, in fact, that the casual or uninformed listener might have only heard some nicely arranged words about how things are different down here in the Deep South. But this is 1963, and Dr. King has stood on the Mall and shared his dream. And the changes that everyone knows must come—will come—and in fact have been gradually coming through the organic processes of generational change and in small, hard-fought legislative increments are arriving much too slowly to suit the rest of the nation.

The movement that had begun back in 1955 with the Montgomery Bus Boycott had swelled into the massive March on Washington just three months before this broadcast. A nation's conscience was pricked and raw. And recently, federal judges—unencumbered by the wishes of constituents or voters—had been stepping in to do in grand sweeps what the state and federal legislatures were too divided to do in anything but baby steps.

Paul mentions none of this in the commentary that follows. But it is there, quietly in the background.

This is Savannah, Georgia. It has been seven years since I was last here. Some cities to which you return after a year or so are hardly recognizable anymore. Everything is uncomfortably unfamiliar. In Savannah, everything is comfortably familiar.

Oh, there is some newness hereabouts . . . big upgrading of port facilities. But in Savannah, the emphasis . . . is not on . . . newness.

I spent last week in our nation's hard-riding, hairy-chested Southwest, out where men are men and everything has to be the newest and the biggest and the most expensive to be the best. This is Savannah, Georgia, where women are ladies and nothing else is worth hardly anything at all unless it is more than a hundred years old.

Where the new West is stimulating, the old South is refreshing. If the skylines are lower, the pace . . . is slower, the pressures . . . are less. Here and now, as seven years ago, there is most interest in the restoration and preservation of ancient landmarks.

I'll be speaking here tomorrow night to a Freedom Forum in Savannah's city auditorium . . . between now and then, looking about and listening and relaxing at the parklike atmosphere of a city where the streets detour around . . . the trees.

Here, as elsewhere, Dixie is wrestling with its conscience these days. Here, where tradition is almost everything, the philosophical tradition is "conservative," the political tradition is "Democrat," and the two are on a collision course. Everybody

*still wants to be conservative. Everybody still wants to be a
Democrat. And you can't be both anymore.*

*It's a hurtful thing for an outsider to watch. It spawns
compromise on the one hand and extremism on the other.*

*Here where a piece of furniture is made more precious by the
scuffs and scars which are the patina of time, folks prefer their
country, and their political party and their society . . . imperfect.
Without modification . . . modernization . . . homogenization.*

They don't think their old Constitution needs a Formica top.

*You familiar with the Route 66 television program? The
cast and crew of this TV show are on location in Savannah
this week. I have breakfast with most of them in the mornings.
They're shooting scenes for upcoming episodes and getting an
early start these days because all of 'em want to take a little time
off for Christmas if they can.*

*But as I say, they're shooting scenes for their television
program around the town, upsetting nobody. I mean the stars
and the starlets of the series go about their playacting almost
unnoticed. Or arousing only the most casual curiosity.*

This . . . is Savannah, Georgia, . . . and it always will be.

Viewed through the twenty-twenty hindsight lens of our twenty-
first century sensibilities, it is certainly possible to see in this a defense
of segregation and institutionalized discrimination. But that is an
uncharitable reading. More accurately, this is Paul Harvey being a
conservative in the classic, purest sense of the word—advocating the
conserving of some things that are good and noble and vital. The
conservative impulse is to caution against throwing out the heirloom
furniture in a frenzy to have the latest and the greatest.

Nevertheless, principled conservatives—particularly those who
were vigilant against the pull to remake America in the image of a European socialist state—found themselves taking some uncomfortable

positions and siding with some unsavory characters as the civil rights movement gained momentum.

Certainly in 1963 the nation had many individuals with the evil of racism living in their hearts who made lots of noise about "states' rights" and "judicial tyranny" in the course of trying to defend the indefensible. But that didn't change the fact that the rights of states under a government of "enumerated powers" and the Constitution's separation of powers provisions were profoundly meaningful concepts that mattered to the health and strength of our republic.

Passionately held antisocialist principles led conservatives of the day such as Paul Harvey, William F. Buckley Jr., Barry Goldwater, and Ronald Reagan to criticize the nationwide use of the federal courts to enact the ideals of the civil rights movement. A year later, conservative principles would compel these same men to oppose President Johnson's sweeping "War on Poverty" welfare legislation. As conservative economist Milton Friedman famously quipped about Johnson's plan, "When you start paying people to be poor, you wind up with an awful lot of poor people!"[4]

Looking back decades later, many principled conservatives would profess that history had shown them to have been absolutely right about the War on Poverty but wrong about the civil rights movement. It seems Paul would have counted himself among them.

Paul's personal observations about Savannah in this 1963 newscast then transition to "Page Three." The pace picks up considerably here. And as before, from our vantage point in the twenty-first century, the headlines and place names take on much fuller significance than would have been possible for the casual 1963 listener:

> *Here is a potpourri of the day's news from Page Three:*
> *Oh! In Nashville, Tennessee, Albert Henry Stone fell asleep*
> *at the wheel and his car ran through a busy intersection and*
> *jumped a curb and tore down a fence and bounced off three*

buildings before it stalled out. Do you know, Henry's unhurt . . .
but awake!

Another thing you might have missed, there's a note on a
place mat in a restaurant in Covington, Kentucky, which says,
quote: 4,076 people, last year, died of "gas" . . . twenty-nine
inhaled it; forty-seven put a match to it; and four thousand
"stepped on it."

Yes, the man who nearly died behind the wheel in 1950 was ever
after a cheerful scold about the need to drive safely.

In Tampa, Florida, President Kennedy predicts that you and
I will fly, ROUTINELY . . . you and I will fly in space at
fifteen thousand miles an hour! He predicts metro planes taking
off from the downtown heart of a city . . . from the crowded
center of the city . . . within eleven years!?

President Kennedy's optimistic predictions didn't quite material-
ize. But forty-five years later, the space tourism industry does seem
poised to take off—at least for the ultrarich.

Baghdad. Another scalp on Nasser's belt. The government of
Iraq has been seized by that nation's armed forces. They've
thrown out the Baath Party and they're moving now to merge
with Syria and the UAR.

Yes, Iraq was in the news in 1963. Egyptian dictator Gamal Abdel
Nasser's attempt to form a transnational Arab superstate by joining
Egypt, Syria, and Iraq didn't last long. The indigenous Baath Party,
inspired and modeled after Nazi Germany's national socialists, would
regain control of Iraq and eventually be led by a man named Saddam

Hussein. And the Middle East's politics and religious rivalries would remain a thorn in the flesh of the world.

After this story, Paul Harvey reads this single-line news item:

An American army sergeant killed in South Vietnam, the seventy-sixth American to die in . . . that war.

"That war." After Paul Harvey died, virtually every obituary mentioned that he had been an early supporter of the Vietnam War but had reversed his position in 1970 in a famous broadcast in which he directly addressed Richard Nixon. The truth about the man's view of Vietnam is much more complicated than that, as we will see in the next chapter. But here in 1963, the newsman who in 1950 had been a skeptic about sending American boys off to die in Korea under a UN flag takes the time to bring our attention to the sacrifice of a single U.S. soldier.

Then, a brief mention of how Venice, Italy, cherished for its Renaissance architecture, is getting "a new civic hospital to be designed by a specialist in ultramodern architecture." As usual, Harvey doesn't tell us what he thinks about this. But we can guess.

He closes, as always, with a humorous news item or anecdote headlined by the words, "Now in our 'For What It's Worth' department. . . ." On this day we learn of a New Zealand woman who lost an expensive diamond ring and filed an insurance claim. Her claim was promptly paid, but a year later, a Mr. Muir at the insurance company received a letter from the woman stating that she had found her ring! He was delighted, of course, because his company would be seeing a return of several thousands of dollars. As Paul Harvey tells it:

The woman said she had found the ring . . . so she did NOT think it was fair to keep the money which the insurance company had paid her . . . so she had donated the money to the Boy Scouts!

Then, at fifteen minutes after noon, as the second hand of the clock is two ticks away from twelve on November 18, 1963, we hear four more words spoken with a crack of a laugh in the voice. "Paul Harvey . . . Good day!"

And history rolls on.

CHAPTER 9

THE GREAT UNRAVELING

"Just by turning to the Left . . . the world has gone in circles."

PAUL HARVEY
The Testing Time (1973)

IT IS SAID THAT THE SIXTIES DIDN'T OFFICIALLY BEGIN until 1964. The thought is that until that year, the culture and sensibilities of the 1950s still dominated. That was before the Beatles stepped off a plane in New York's Kennedy Airport and were greeted by three thousand screaming fans. Up until then, Elvis—the patriotic boy from Tupelo, Mississippi, who had happily put on a military uniform at the height of his popularity—had reigned as king.

Now, something utterly new was on the scene. Change, of a harsh and revolutionary kind, was in the air.

Others argue that the innocence of the 1950s actually died on a bright November Friday one year before—in a noontime motorcade through downtown Dallas.

• • •

Four days after his broadcast from Savannah, Georgia, Paul Harvey has run through his daily routine precisely as usual—up until 12:36 p.m., anyway:

Rising at 3:30 a.m., he quickly dresses in slacks, shirt, tie, and sport coat. He is occasionally teased about "dressing up for radio," but he doesn't care. When he first started in the business, no self-respecting man would have considered showing up for work without a jacket and tie. In later years, as trends would bring a much more relaxed atmosphere to radio newsrooms, Paul would briefly try the shirtsleeves and open collar approach. But one day after a broadcast his longtime engineer for *Paul Harvey News and Comment,* Bob Benninghoff, would offhandedly mention, "You're starting to sound as casual as you dress." That would do it.

After a quick bowl of oatmeal, he makes the short drive into downtown Chicago to the studios of ABC Radio News at the corner of Wacker Drive and Michigan Avenue. The wire services and newspapers are scoured for material for the morning's first broadcast, the five-minute newscast at 9:00 a.m. that will be fed to more than 1,200 radio stations around the country and four hundred or so Armed Forces Network affiliates around the globe. On this morning, as on most mornings in the latter half of the twentieth century, more Americans will hear Paul than any other person in broadcasting.

Once at a 1991 New York City luncheon to honor Billy Graham, Paul was present, as were the top three network television news anchors—Tom Brokaw, Dan Rather, and Peter Jennings. There, ABC's Leonard Goldenson was speaking and had the temerity to point out that Paul Harvey spoke to more people on most days than either Rather, Jennings, or Brokaw. Peter Jennings added loudly, "Combined." And everyone in the room laughed.[1]

By 7:30 a.m., Angel has arrived and has joined the production process. At five minutes before 9:00 a.m., the engineer cues up the *William Tell Overture,* more familiar to children of the 1950s and 1960s as the theme from *The Lone Ranger.* This is Paul's cue to begin those vocal warm-up exercises learned from Miss Ronan back at

Tulsa's Central High those many years ago. *Ngonga-ngonga-ngonga . . . Wolf-one-two-three-four . . .*

Once the nine o'clock newscast is complete, work begins on the longer, fifteen-minute version that will air at noon. On this day, one of the big stories making headlines is President Kennedy's two-day whirlwind tour of Texas and the internal squabbling going on there between the liberal and moderate wings of the state Democratic Party. Ralph Yarborough, the liberal U.S. senator from Texas, was furious at being left off a presidential dinner invitation list by the more conservative Democrat Governor John Connally.

Paul delivers his second newscast of the day, finishing precisely at 12:15. At that moment, President John F. Kennedy's motorcade is making its way from Love Field Airport toward downtown Dallas. It is running a few minutes behind because Kennedy stopped the procession twice—once to shake hands with some nuns who had gathered along the route and then again to greet some schoolchildren.

At 12:39, Dallas listeners of station KLIF hear the song "I Have a Boyfriend" by The Chiffons interrupted by the station's "bulletin alert" sounder—a frightening, high-pitched alarm that sounds like an air-raid warning. Over the jarring sound of the tone, KLIF reporter Gary DeLaune delivers this terse announcement:

> *This KLIF Bulletin from Dallas: Three shots reportedly were fired at the motorcade of President Kennedy today near the downtown section. KLIF News is checking out the report; we will have further reports. Stay tuned.*

This is the first anyone in America outside of Dealey Plaza learns that something awful has happened in Dallas.

At the ABC Radio News studios in Chicago, the wire-service bell begins to ring, and the Teletype clacks: "URGENT: Shots fired at presidential motorcade." Everyone there quickly gathers near the network news-feed speakers as an engineer turns up the volume. Across the country, those listening to ABC Radio Network affiliates are about to become the first Americans outside of Dallas to get the news. At 12:36 p.m., ABC's Don Gardiner interrupts Doris Day's "Hooray for Hollywood":

> *We interrupt this program to bring you a special bulletin from ABC Radio. Here is a special bulletin from Dallas, Texas. Three shots were fired at President Kennedy's motorcade today in downtown Dallas, Texas. This is ABC Radio. To repeat: In Dallas, Texas, three shots were fired at President Kennedy's motorcade today, the president now making a two-day speaking tour of Texas. We're going to stand by for more details on the incident in Dallas; stay tuned to your ABC station for further details. Now we return you to your regular program.*

Like every other news reporter in America, and every other American for that matter, Paul spends the rest of the afternoon following the flow of information out of Dallas as rumor-fueled confusion gradually gives way to shock, then to grief, and eventually to anger. In those first hours, there is also real fear. Officials within the government and inside the press corps privately wonder if the assassination is a precursor to a full-scale Soviet attack.

At some point that afternoon, Paul gets word from New York to prepare a special evening edition of *News and Comment*. So as he has done for every other newscast, once he feels he has all the information that is going to be available, he sits down at a typewriter and taps out his report.

He once said, "The years don't always add wisdom, but they add perspective." So, when it comes time to speak to a grief-shocked nation in the midst of a national crisis, his first instinct is to help us find perspective. His opening paragraph is simply a reminder that this is not the first time we've lost a president to an assassin's bullet. In essence: "We've been here before. We'll get through it."

The balance of the five-minute broadcast is a masterpiece of concision. That evening, Howard K. Smith is helping to anchor ABC's coverage for both television and radio. At the appointed time, Smith throws to Paul, and we hear:

> *Good evening, Americans.*
> *We are just never ready for this KIND of thing in this country. We deplore the hotheads elsewhere in the world who change governments with guns, but we try to ignore the fact that now four of our own presidents have been cut down by assassins.*

Over the next several minutes, Harvey crisply, tersely recounts the known facts about the day's events in sequence. Then, true to form, he takes a moment to point out the duplicity of the Soviet Union:

> *And it's significant to ME that Moscow radio hastened to say today that our president had been killed today by extreme Right-wing elements. Now it develops the assassin's allegiance was Red. He wore a brown shirt, uniform of a Castro Communist terrorist, and he, Lee Oswald, is the chairman of the pro-Castro outfit called the "Fair Play for Cuba Committee."*

It is not surprising that among the hundreds of condolences expressed that day, Harvey chooses to share some thoughts delivered by one of his heroes:

> *General Douglas MacArthur, in a telegram to Mrs. Kennedy tonight, said, quote: I realize the utter futility of words at such a time. But as a former comrade-in-arms, his death . . . kills something within me.*

Paul pauses briefly to regain his composure. Then he presses on to the conclusion of his report:

> *The president's special car has a bulletproof bubble-glass top,*
> *but the top was down today so he could wave to the enthusiastic*
> *crowds. The Dallas reception was the most enthusiastic of any*
> *stop in Texas. For weeks a big debate raged about which of the*
> *city's luminaries would get to sit at the head table this noon.*
> *Nobody did.*
>
> *And on the president's White House desk are the calls and*
> *the callers and documents and the urgent things to be done—*
> *which could not POSSIBLY await his attention for another*
> *day. But they will wait now.*
>
> *It is for us that one must grieve tonight . . . for a generation*
> *which has so refined its intellect that it can split atoms and*
> *communicate with the moon, and yet remains at the mercy of*
> *its own undisciplined emotions.*
>
> *If the world is one day destroyed it will come just like this,*
> *you know. It'll not be the H-bomb that did it. It'll be the greed*
> *. . . or the . . . fear . . . or the hate that set it off.*
>
> *Paul Harvey . . . good night.*

To many Americans of Paul Harvey's generation, it couldn't help but feel that as the 1960s unfolded, the fabric of our nation unraveled. The escalation of the Vietnam War, something Paul had deeply mixed emotions about, seemed to come with a corresponding decline in morals and restraint. A culture of protest and dissent—born in part of legitimate indignation over civil rights affronts like Jim Crow and segregation—seemed to metastasize into a large-scale movement to tear down everything preceding generations had built. And to reject everything they held sacred. Seemingly everything was subject to protest, but nothing galvanized it or fueled it like "the war."

Although there was never more than a noisy minority of young people at the forefront, at the time it seemed to Americans over thirty that the whole world had turned upside down. Police were reviled and referred to as "pigs." Illicit drug use was pandemic and celebrated in song and story. And the sexual mores that had defined civilized society were tossed aside.

For more literary elders, it brought to mind the most famous passage of William Butler Yeats's poem "The Second Coming":

> *Things fall apart; the centre cannot hold;*
> *Mere anarchy is loosed upon the world,*
> *The blood-dimmed tide is loosed, and everywhere*
> *The ceremony of innocence is drowned;*
> *The best lack all conviction, while the worst*
> *Are full of passionate intensity.*

It is no wonder that at one point during this period, Paul spoke for three entire generations of adult Americans when he said he felt like "a displaced person" in his own country.

On May 5, 1965, the University of California at Berkeley was the site of the first of many draft-card burnings that took place around the country. On this day, a coffin was marched to the Berkeley draft board. Protests, sit-ins, teach-ins, and the like continued through the summer. President Lyndon Johnson responded in August by signing a new law attaching up to a five-year prison sentence or a ten-thousand-dollar fine to the criminal act of burning a draft card. But the protests and burnings only intensified.

As we've seen, Paul was universally perceived in later years to have been a strong supporter of the Vietnam War prior to 1970. A review of his commentaries and columns in the 1960s does not bear out this view.

He believed, as he had stated during the Korean War, that not a single drop of American blood should be spilled in a war the nation and its leaders had no will to win. It seemed clear to him early in the Vietnam War that we didn't have the will to engage in the total war that was necessary to win that conflict. For example, in an April 20, 1967, installment of *Paul Harvey News and Comment*, we hear him say:

> *And while you slept our navy's planes bombed closer to the heart of Haiphong Harbor than ever before. Our planes from the carrier* Kitty Hawk *attacked two thermal stations two miles from Haiphong. Through the port of Haiphong flows 60 percent of all the enemies' war-making material. These two plants we hit furnish power to the port area and to a cement factory. It is clear that we are trying to cripple the port . . . without clobbering it. Trying to turn the lights out without sinking all those enemy supply ships, so many of which . . . are British ships.*
>
> *Russian MiGs are now coming up after our planes over North Vietnam. A swarm of seventeen MiG-17 interceptors took off from those air bases which we are NOT bombing. We shot down one.*

Paul wasn't the only one with a sense that bureaucratic and political concerns were trumping sound military strategy. Just a couple of months after this broadcast, another aircraft carrier—the *Forrestal*—began a similar bombing campaign over North Vietnam called Operation Rolling Thunder. One of the pilots on that ship was a thirty-year-old flier named John McCain. But as he would later relate in his biography, *Faith of My Fathers*, McCain and his fellow pilots quickly became exasperated by micromanagement from Washington. He wrote, "In all candor, we thought our civilian commanders were complete idiots who didn't have the least notion of what it took to win the war."[2]

It was this tendency of Washington to send America's finest men to fight with one arm tied behind their backs that Paul simply could not abide. And in this he is, as always, a faithful reflection of the great, silent mass of Middle Americans. He, and they, continued to have serious concerns about Soviet expansionism around the world. And if their political leaders told them there was a fight in Southeast Asia that was vital to U.S. interests to wage, it was their first instinct to believe them and be supportive. But they expected it to be fought to win—as quickly and as efficiently as possible.

In 1966, Paul still seemed to be holding out some small hope that President Johnson and the Pentagon would adopt a military strategy for victory, win the thing, and bring our boys home—all before rapidly eroding public support started causing Congress to go wobbly. Events would eventually show that these hopes were in vain.

We were also told in obituaries that Paul was an unwavering, uncritical supporter of military spending. This, too, is belied by the broadcaster's own words. In a 1966 newscast, he almost audibly rolls his eyes at a new Pentagon request for funding:

> *Americans, your Pentagon has asked Congress for more than two-and-a-half BILLION dollars in new military construction in the United States and elsewhere. With all . . . (laughs) with all the bases and installations we've been closing up and shutting down . . . (laughing) now they're planning two-and-a-half billion in NEW construction.*

Perhaps the broadcaster was perceived as a full-throated hawk on Vietnam simply because he was so openly disgusted by the words and actions of the people who were protesting it. In that April 1967 broadcast, Paul gives voice to the frustrations of millions of Middle

Americans weary of hearing their country torn down by young, spoiled products of privilege when he reports:

> *Washington. A likeness of draft director General Lewis Hershey has been burned on the campus of Howard University. In next Sunday's* Washington Star, *though, some back talk for the beatniks. Catholic war veterans are picturing the demonstrators as . . . as what most of them are . . . in Sunday's* Star. *And maybe it is time . . . for some protest by . . . yes, for some protest by . . . PRO-Americans.*

You have to love that line: "some backtalk for the beatniks." And you can be sure that when it came through radio speakers—in barbershops and machine shops and kitchens and cars all over America—heads were nodding in agreement.

Beginning in 1968, heads would be nodding in living rooms each evening across America, as well. A syndicated five-minute television program called *Paul Harvey Comments* launched with Angel producing. It would enjoy a twenty-year run. Hundreds of local ABC television affiliates ran the program as an element in their evening newscasts. This is the television program that gave many baby boomers their first exposure to Paul Harvey.

●   ●   ●

For Paul, the 1960s weren't all about chronicling a great nation's decay and decadence. For inspired relief there was the excitement and pride engendered by the space race. President Kennedy's first address to Congress had set forth the challenge of putting an American on the moon before decade's end. Each year seemed to bring that prize closer to our grasp. And you would have been hard-pressed to find a ten-year-old boy anywhere in America more filled with gee-whiz wonder at each milestone than Paul.

On May 31, 1966, he reports the landing of NASA's *Surveyor 1* probe, saying:

> *Our fancy gizmo landed on the moon last night! Softly, safely, and intact. Developed a malfunction which was repaired from Pasadena, California. And it's now sending back pictures! And sometime after midnight tonight will, on command from earth, take out its little toylike shovel and start digging.*

Of course, it was the Apollo missions toward the end of the decade that truly captured the world's imagination. After the broadcaster's passing, Chicago newsman Phil Rogers wrote that some of his most fond and vivid Paul Harvey memories are of the commentaries he heard from his home in Oklahoma. One that aired when Rogers was twelve stood out even after many years. It was a *Rest of the Story* that "extolled the virtues of a young man who dreamed of flying," Rogers wrote. "The last line: 'And tomorrow, that young man, will set foot . . . upon . . . the Moon.' What does it say to you that I can still quote it?"[3]

That first moon landing took place early on Richard Nixon's watch. The new president had inherited a situation in Vietnam that presented few good options. The protest movement was growing and intensifying; the news media was largely sympathetic to the protestors and hostile to the effort; the American people were weary; and Congress, sensitive to all of these factors, was prepared to start placing severe restrictions on the executive branch's ability to conduct a successful war.

Paul was, and always had been, of the conviction that wars should be fought only if necessary and only to win. When that clearly became impossible, Paul did something that shocked many people.

On May 1, 1970—ironically the traditional socialist holiday of May Day—Paul spoke of President Nixon's stated plan to expand the war into Cambodia and said, "Mr. President, I love you. But you're wrong." He went on to call for an end to the Vietnam War.

History apparently views this announcement as some sort of reversal or change of heart. But it was not. It was a resignation—a feeling perfectly consistent with the values and principles Paul held all his life.

Yes, he was now calling for the very same thing radical activists like Tom Hayden, Jane Fonda, and Abbie Hoffman had been calling for, but for starkly different reasons. Paul thought too much of the blood of American servicemen to spill one more drop in a noble but lost cause. The activists, on the other hand, actually believed their country was helping the wrong side.

Decades later, Larry King asked him about that broadcast:

> I had always been reared with the old MacArthur feeling that the only excuse for getting into a war is to win it. The only justification for war is to win it. And then, one day, I realized that in spite of the expenditure of all of our gold and all of that blood, in Vietnam and in Korea, the most we were able to deliver was a stalemate on the fifty-yard line.
>
> We'd paid much too high a price for that. And it was then that I suggested that we drive it or park it.[4]

Many believe it was on that very day that Richard Nixon began working on a plan for withdrawal from Vietnam. We don't know for sure. What we do know is that by the time Paul got back to his desk about an hour after the broadcast, his assistant rushed up to tell him something.

"Mr. Harvey . . . the phone. It's the White House."

CHAPTER 10

THE DECADE
OF DOUBT

*"I am a salesman. And until the day they nail the lid on that box,
I will be. And until that day, my primary focus will be keeping
our God-blessed United States of America sold . . . on itself."*

PAUL HARVEY

IT IS SUNDAY MORNING, AND PAUL HARVEY steers a rental car northward and upward along a winding road outside of Phoenix. Angel takes in the desert scenery from the passenger seat. It is 1971, and Chicago's winter snows have brought the couple to Phoenix for a brief vacation.

While exploring, the couple drives into the small community of Cave Creek, about ten miles north of Phoenix's northern edge. Paul, the history buff, has already learned that Cave Creek holds the distinction of being Arizona's oldest town. That alone makes it worth a visit. There they spot a tiny, white, steeple-topped, clapboard-sided church perched on an isolated hill just off the road. They think it quite charming, see worshipers arriving, and so on a whim, decide to make the service a part of their morning.

Paul, a big-city dweller for over twenty-five years now, has never stopped craving the simplicity of small-town things and the company of small-town people. No matter where they are, the inseparable couple rarely fails to attend church on Sunday morning.

Indeed, from every outward appearance, Paul is the personification of a Christian man. He is deeply moral, in public and in private. He is a devoted student of the Bible, quoting its verses and deploying its imagery frequently in his commentaries, columns, and books. He and Angel are a fountain of good works, giving freely and frequently to an astonishing array of charities and ministries. And there had been that very real watershed moment of belief and consecration back at that Kansas bedside all those years ago . . . a moment in which John 3:16 went from being a familiar quote to an invitation accepted. And yet . . .

"Something was missing," Paul would explain a year later. "There was a vague emptiness in my life; an incompleteness that I could not define."[1] Paul had never been satisfied that he had the kind of relationship with God he ought to possess. He had a tendency to worry and fret over small things, and he knew such apprehensiveness should have no place in the life of a person whose trust was in God. He was also aware of a willfulness . . . a stubborn hardness on the inside that he suspected was not pleasing to his Lord.

It was his practice to pray each morning as he cruised along Lake Shore Drive at 4:30 a.m. But more and more he found these prayer times devolving into an inward wrestling match with his own sensitive conscience: "Often on the dark, deserted expressway I would seem to hear God's plan for the day. But by the time I was halfway downtown, I'd be arguing with Him, making exceptions, bending His directions."[2] The Paul who walked through those church doors that Sunday was a man grown weary of the inner struggle to be a better Christian.

On this day, Paul and Angel slip in the back door of the little church and find roughly a dozen people seated and chatting on wooden folding chairs. With an upright piano positioned front left and a wooden pulpit front and center, it looks like many of the small Tulsa churches Paul visited as a boy. The tourists take a seat in the back and, in vain, try to be inconspicuous.

After a few familiar hymns, the pastor introduces a visiting minister who will be doing the preaching that day. When the man begins his sermon, his grammar is that of an uneducated man, and his speaking style is plain and unpolished. After a few minutes, Angel looks sideways at her husband, expecting to catch his gaze and a facial expression that indicates he thinks this has been a mistake and wants to slip out the back door. But she doesn't. In fact, Paul seems to be hanging on every word.

The topic this day is baptism. And this being a Baptist church, the preacher doesn't mean the sprinkling of infants as was the practice at the Aurandts' Presbyterian church in Tulsa when Paul was born. No, it means full-body, soaking-wet immersion of adults and youngsters old enough to know they are choosing to follow Christ—just as Paul's Anabaptist ancestors in Pennsylvania and Germany had practiced.

With simple country eloquence that touches Paul's soul, the preacher speaks of how profoundly alone a man is without a heavenly Father and how we can only find real purpose and peace through a total surrender to him. *But haven't I already done this?* Paul thinks. The minister goes on to explain that there is a second step, a step of obedience in baptism. "There is no magic in the water," he adds. "One's immersion is simply an act of obedience, a sign of total submission to God."[3]

Those final words send Paul's mind running. As he would later recall:

> *Submission to God.* I twisted on my chair. New understanding discomfited me. Long years ago I had asked to be saved but had I offered to serve? I began to realize how much of *me* I had been holding back. Could this be the source of my uneasiness, the inconsistency within me?[4]

Soon the sermon concludes with something that is familiar to anyone who has ever attended a Baptist church service. The *invitation.* "If there is anyone here who would like to take this step and be baptized, come forward now," the preacher says.

Paul finds himself on his feet and moving toward the man in front of the pulpit. This church has no baptismal tank of its own, so the pastor arranges for Paul to be baptized that very evening at the baptismal pond of a church down in the valley.

Make of it what you will, but Paul's unambiguous testimony would be that he came up out of that pond water a different man:

> The preacher had said there was nothing magic in the water. Yet as I descended into its depths and rose again, I knew something life changing had happened. . . . Afterward, I cried like a baby, a kind of release I suppose. I remember looking at Angel and her eyes were shining. She knew well what this meant to me, for she had been blessed with the same experience as a girl.[5]

He would claim that from this day forward his lifelong tendency toward worry and fretfulness is gone. He would feel more genuine joy more consistently. He also would become much less self-conscious when talking about his faith. He theorized it was because "baptism is such a public act . . . one's dignity gets as drenched as one's body."

Thirty-two years later Larry King asked Paul about this experience. The broadcaster told the host the story of the little white church on the hill in Arizona's oldest town and said, "And boy, that's where the fun begins . . . when you stop tearing yourself in half."[6]

Paul may have found internal calm in 1971, but the country did not manage to follow him. Instead, America went right on tearing herself apart.

Since the 1960s had gotten off to a late start, it seems the turbulent decade felt entitled to spill over into the first few years of the 1970s. Indeed, the dark clouds that had been gathering throughout the 1960s—social unrest, disaffection with the war, the sexual revolution, and the recreational use of illegal drugs—seemed to break out into full-blown thunderstorms in these years.

Of course, most Americans over thirty, as well as most young people in Southern and Midwestern states, still held the same God-and-country values they had inherited from their parents. For this "silent majority," as Richard Nixon had described it in 1969, simply watching the nightly news or reading the newspaper had become an exercise in infuriation. Every protestor's display of the Vietcong flag, every vitriolic denunciation of America as evil, every picket sign saying "Cops are pigs" fueled this righteous indignation.

The fact was, many of these patriotic Americans had their own reservations about the war and especially about how it was being conducted. But they deplored the counterculture's message, methods, and morals. Thus, it wasn't so much that they were enthusiastically pro-war as they were enthusiastically anti-antiwar.

When Merle Haggard released his song "Okie from Muskogee" in 1969, he reportedly meant the song to be satirical. But it became a huge hit for him precisely because Middle America didn't take it that way. They took the song to heart because they didn't "burn our draft cards down on Main Street." They did "still wave Old Glory down at the courthouse." And they did "like livin' right and bein' free." Haggard had expressed what they were feeling in a single song. But they counted on Paul, born just a few miles up the road from Muskogee, to give voice to their values and their frustrations six days a week.

This expectation is what made Paul's "Mr. President, I love you. But you're wrong" broadcast on May 1, 1970, such a shock to so many traditional-values-oriented Americans. In the days following the broadcast, he received an avalanche of more than 24,000 letters—most of them expressing disappointment or bewilderment or anger. Many were from enraged veterans who considered him a traitor to the cause.

More cynical observers wondered if the fact that Paul and Angel's only child, Young Paul, was of draft age had anything to do with the broadcaster's apparent change of position on the war. But there is no evidence for that. In fact, Paul Jr. had been of draft age for three years when that controversial broadcast aired.

It is true that Angel had encouraged her son to register as a conscientious objector (CO) on religious grounds. It is not known whether his father opposed or supported this decision, but this certainly opened him up to a charge of hypocrisy. In 1966, Paul had made much of Muhammad Ali's, aka Cassius Clay's, refusal to submit to the draft and of his claim of CO status on religious grounds. But again, Young Paul's registration as a CO took place several years before that May broadcast. It is reasonable to assume that if it were going to sway his father's position on the war, it would have done so well before 1970.

The facts and the timing of the decision are more consistent with the assessment of Chicago newsman Phil Rogers, who wrote after Paul's death: "He spoke from the heart of middle America. When they waved the flag for the boys in Vietnam, he did too. When they decided they had had enough, it was Mr. Harvey who told Richard Nixon, via his giant audience, that it was time to bring those boys home."[7]

Paul's "bring them home" was just as consistent with his instinctive isolationism as his nuanced support of the war had been with his long-standing anticommunism.

As mentioned at the end of the previous chapter, part of what drove Paul's decision to call for a winding down of the war was his reluctant conclusion that the war would not and could not be fought to a victory. If that view was based in part upon an assumption that erosion of public support was going to accelerate, it turned out to be a sound prediction. A series of high-profile events was about to grab headlines, and none of them helped shore up grassroots backing for continued sacrifice in Southeast Asia.

Just three days later, on May 4, a clash between antiwar protestors and National Guardsmen on the campus of Kent State University in

Ohio left four students dead and nine others wounded, one of those permanently paralyzed. The shootings generated massive media coverage, and in response, hundreds of universities, colleges, and high schools around the country were closed by student strikes involving an estimated 4 million students.

That November, the court-martial of army Lieutenant William Calley and thirteen other army officers began. They were charged in connection with what had become known as the My Lai Massacre—the horrifying details of which had already been the subject of regular news reports for a full year. Now the trials put the grim details back in the forefront of the public's mind once again. Those details included the deaths of between 350 and 500 Vietnamese civilians—many of them women and children—in the villages of My Lai and My Khe on March 16, 1968.

Charges were eventually dropped against most of the officers, and of those who stood trial, only Calley was convicted.

To those who viewed America as the unjust aggressor in Vietnam, these allegations seemed an overwhelming validation of all their assumptions. To them, Calley was a monster who stood as a proxy for the monstrosity of the war. But to others, Calley looked more like a scapegoat. From their vantage point, it seemed as if the army was bowing to the pressure of a virtual lynch mob stirred up by antiwar activists and a sympathetic media. Paul shared that view.

By the time Calley's conviction was issued, the officer had already received twenty-five personal letters from Paul Harvey. In the first of these, Paul wrote, "I have every confidence that you are a fine military officer that we can all be proud of."[8] These notes weren't a publicity ploy or an attempt to sway public opinion. Paul never intended that the public even be aware of them. The letters were simply heartfelt expressions of support and encouragement from one American to a soldier he believed had been thrust into an impossible situation, had done the best he could, and was getting a raw deal.

Paul was far from the only prominent person to view Calley sympathetically. The sitting governor of Georgia—a fellow by the name of Jimmy Carter—instituted American Fighting Man's Day in response and asked Georgians to drive for a week with their headlights on. Indiana's governor suggested that all state flags should be flown at half-staff for the convicted soldier. The governors of Utah and Mississippi also expressed their disappointment with the verdict. The state legislatures of Arkansas, Kansas, Texas, New Jersey, and South Carolina all went on record requesting clemency for Calley. A Gallup Poll taken immediately after the trial revealed that 79 percent of Americans disagreed with the Calley verdict.

The war would continue to be a flash point for division and resentment within America for several more years. In that span, Jane Fonda would make her infamous trip to Hanoi and have a photo op with a North Vietnamese antiaircraft gun. Nixon would travel to China. Palestinian terrorists would kidnap and kill eleven Israeli athletes at the Summer Olympics in Munich. And Richard Nixon would win reelection in a landslide over George McGovern, although Democratic majorities would be retained in both houses of Congress. Many of those newly elected Democrats had run on a platform of opposition to the war.

The year 1973 witnessed the end of U.S. combat operations in Vietnam. The war was over—for us, anyway. Not so much for our former allies. Twenty-five thousand additional South Vietnamese were killed just during the short-lived, Kissinger-negotiated "ceasefire" that permitted U.S. withdrawal. Before the fall of Saigon, hundreds of thousands of others would die. Afterward, countless others would either flee or be rounded up into "reeducation camps."

• • •

The end of the war left Americans to focus their attention on a host of problems that festered here at home. Inflation was running high, as was unemployment. Gasoline price shocks and shortages were on the horizon. The activist Left turned its energies to issues such as the environment and women's rights. And there was an unfolding news story that wouldn't go away about some sort of break-in during the presidential campaign—at the Watergate building in Washington, D.C.

To most of Paul Harvey's audience, it seemed America's downward slide toward something unwholesome and unhealthy was continuing, even accelerating. Some were beginning to believe that their country's greatest days were behind them.

It was to this audience and to combat this pessimism—what President Jimmy Carter would later call a "malaise"—that Paul resurrected and updated a speech he had given frequently in the late 1950s. It was titled "The Testing Time." In 1960, Word Records, the Christian label headquartered in Waco, Texas, had even released the speech on a vinyl record album by the same name. In 1973, with growing fear about the economy fueling public demands for the government to do something, the themes of "The Testing Time" seemed timely once again. In classic Paul Harvey style, this verbal essay covers a wide range of topics, but at its core, it is an exhortation to Americans to "remain strong . . . in our arms and in our hearts."

In tone and content it is equal parts sermon, pep talk, and grandfatherly lecture. Paul's aim is clearly to make a case to working-class Americans for free enterprise and self-reliance—warning them against the liberty-robbing seduction of looking to the government for rescue. He delivers his case in a masterpiece of that "shirtsleeve English" he learned reading William Allen White—the sage of Emporia.

He begins by reminding us, as he did in other moments of national crisis or upset, that we've been here before and that there is nothing new under the sun. He uses parables, *Rest of the Story*–styled anecdotes from history, and good old-fashioned evangelistic preaching to make points about evils such as the insidious nature of redistribution of wealth through taxation:

*But you know it was for us, the American people, to become
the first in recorded history ever voluntarily to surrender our
rights to private property? Oh, yes we did. With an innocent-
sounding constitutional amendment, the sixteenth, which says
that "Congress shall have the power to lay and collect taxes
on incomes, from whatever source derived." And we forgot to
put any limits on the extent to which we could tax ourselves.
Conceivably, we could be taxed out of all private property . . .
we could awaken one morning and find that the government
owns the farm and the house and car and has a mortgage on
the church—legally!*

*Historically, whenever any nation has taxed its people
more than 25 percent of their national income, initiative was
destroyed and that nation was headed for economic eclipse.*

Paul also warns us about the runaway growth of government:

*At first there appears to be nothing wrong with asking
government to perform some extra service for you, but if you ask
government for extra services, government, in order to perform
its increasing function, has to get bigger, right?*

*And as government gets bigger, in order to support its
increasing size, it has to what? Tax the individual more.
So the individual gets littler.*

*And to collect the increased taxes requires more tax
collectors, so the government gets bigger, and in order to pay the
additional tax collectors it has to tax the individual more, so
the government gets bigger and the individual gets littler. And
the government gets bigger. And the individual gets littler.*

*Until the government is all-powerful, and the individual
is hardly anything at all.*

*Until the government is all-powerful and the people
are cattle.*

He ever and always viewed the greatest threat to America to be
not an attack from outside but rather a slow internal surrender by her
people to the illusory seduction of the welfare state. He warns that the
temptation to swap liberty for false comfort is a fool's bargain.

*I am satisfied with all my heart that if Uncle Sam ever does get
whipped, it will have been an inside job. It was internal decay,
not external attack, that destroyed the Roman Empire.*

What follows is Paul preaching a bootstrap gospel of self-reliance
and faith in God. In an era in which the well-intentioned but mis-
guided welfare programs of the 1960s were already creating an explo-
sion of fatherlessness in America's inner cities, and as "middle-class
welfare" and "corporate welfare" programs were being crafted in
Congress on a weekly basis, Paul calls his fellow Americans back to
the virtues and satisfactions of standing on one's own two feet:

*In this little, bitty instant as historical time is measured, our
7 percent of the earth's population has come to possess more than
half of all the world's good things. How come?*

*Well, sir, when that early pioneer turned his eyes toward
the West, he didn't demand that somebody else look after
him. He didn't demand a free education. He didn't demand
a guaranteed rocking chair at eventide. He didn't demand
that somebody else take care of him if he got ill or got old.
There was an old-fashioned philosophy in those days that
a man was supposed to provide for his own . . . and for his
own future.*

He didn't demand a maximum amount of money for a

minimum amount of work. Nor did he expect pay for no work at all. Come to think of it, he didn't demand anything.

That hard-handed pioneer just looked out there at the rolling plains stretching away to the tall green mountains and then lifted his eyes to the blue skies and said, "Thank you, God. Now I can take it from here."

Then, as ever, Paul's instinct is to balance the stern words of warning with some qualified hope:

Now that spirit isn't dead in our country; it's dormant, it's been discredited in some circles, driven underground, but it isn't dead. It's just that a few seasons ago politicians, baiting their hooks with free barbecue and trading a Ponzi promise for votes, began telling us we don't want opportunity anymore, we want security. We don't want opportunity, they said; we want security. And they said it so often we came to believe them.

We wanted security. And they gave us chains. And we were "secure" . . .

If we can revive in ourselves, then in our youth, something of that basic American's creed—the horizon has never ever been so limitless. For man stands now on the threshold of its highest adventure of all, his first faltering footsteps into space. Twenty years from today, half of the products you will be using in your everyday living aren't even in the dictionary yet. We've got it made. If we just keep on keeping on. . . .

History promises only this for certain: We will get exactly what we deserve.

Finally, like a revival evangelist giving an invitation, he invites us all to make a decision and reminds us this brief time on earth is not all there is and that storms are indeed "part of the normal climate of life":

We sometimes think our generation has been especially discriminated against. But in every generation young folks have wondered whether they should pursue an education or take the easiest possible way. Whether they should enter the professions or not. Young folks have wondered whether they should marry, or no. Young marrieds have wondered whether they ought to bring babies into an era of regulation and regimentation. In every hour of history there have been these questions, the same as we have today. Because there have always been storms to . . . to test men.

Americans, a paradise is being prepared somewhere . . . a perfect place. Don't you see, we've got to prove HERE we deserve to be there. . . .

There's an election going on all the time. The Lord votes for you, the devil votes against you, and you cast the deciding vote.

His final words are to those who may not share his views and ideals. To them he extends an invitation to come together in agreement on the proposition that the sweat and sacrifice of our forefathers are worthy of honor:

If, however, you do not share my personal conviction concerning this testing time, if the gravy train running three sections and factory whistles summoning three shifts are creating too much din for a still, small voice to be heard . . . let us nonetheless with the conscience of reasonable men preserve and protect and defend this last great green and precious place on earth against all its enemies . . . foreign and domestic, so help us God . . . if only because so many people you never knew have broken their hearts to get it . . . and to keep it for you.

These reminders and encouragements would prove timely, because as the 1970s rolled on, so did the shocks to the national psyche.

Throughout 1973, the Watergate scandal continued to roil Washington and the nation. The Chinese water torture effect of the daily revelations of petty crimes, shenanigans, and political paranoia surrounding Richard Nixon and his staff shook the confidence of Middle America to the core.

Paul didn't approve of or excuse any of the Nixon administration's malfeasance or shady actions, and he expressed his disappointment repeatedly on the air. But he also believed a Left-leaning press didn't like the outcome of the previous presidential election and was out to help Democrats in Congress undo the result for which the voters had overwhelmingly voted.

In a New Year's Eve radio interview, Paul explained:

> I think investigative reporting is great insurance for the American people. When somebody, in public office particularly, starts to put something over on us, it's always some nosy newsman who can holler his head off. I think recently, in the case of Watergate, this has been abused. When the watchdog hangs on after the policeman arrives, and just hangs on and hangs on, sinking his teeth in deeper and deeper, then I think the exposé has become a vendetta. Then I think our political motives are suspect. Then what you've got on your hands is a mean dog.[9]

On August 8, 1974, Richard Nixon announced in a nationally televised address that he was resigning effective noon the next day. In later years, Paul would describe the events as a type of "coup" in which an American government was "overthrown."[10]

•   •   •

As the seventies unfolded, Paul's position on Vietnam wasn't the only stand he took that surprised his listeners, perplexed his fellow conservatives, and shocked his heartland fans.

In 1972, for example, Congress voted to send the Equal Rights Amendment (ERA) to the states for ratification. The ERA was a constitutional amendment that would have outlawed all discrimination or preferences on the basis of sex while empowering Congress to make laws applying the letter and spirit of the measure to states, businesses, and private organizations.

The passage gave backers of the amendment seven years to get three-quarters of the country's state legislatures to ratify the measure and thereby amend the U.S. Constitution. An often-bitter state-by-state battle began. And on several occasions over the following years Paul made statements on the air in support of the amendment. Liberal and feminist backers of the initiative were surprised but delighted to have America's most influential commentator's backing.

Had it been any other lifelong Republican, support for the ERA might not have been so surprising. Support for the measure had been a plank in Republican Party platforms since 1944. The measure had been first introduced in Congress in 1923. It had, in fact, been Democrats from the northern states that had traditionally blocked the measure in Congress each year, because the labor unions were strongly against it. But Paul wasn't just any other lifelong Republican. Frankly, it is difficult to square Paul's support for the ERA with his lifetime of passionate, principled opposition to the expansion of government regulation and control over private enterprise.

For three decades he had thundered like an Old Testament prophet against encroachment of government bureaucracies and described constitutional amendments like the sixteenth and seventeenth as "tearing gaping holes in our foundation . . . the Constitution."[11] He had warned, "Every new extension of the domain of government, however they justified it, moved us closer and closer to the brink of the very kind of 'ism' our sons ostensibly have been dying to defeat."[12] And he had written:

The Constitution's Bill of Rights holds individual liberty to be inviolate. A right with which the blueprint . . . the Declaration of Independence . . . says . . .

You and I were *endowed by God.*

We have since, however, granted almost limitless executive authority to the President of the United States. With this power he has regulated and regimented. Then we spent astronomical sums on a sprawling bureaucracy to police the processes.[13]

Yet in his favorable comments toward the ERA, Paul endorsed a change to the Constitution that would arguably have been the most sweeping expansion of government control over business and private enterprise since the New Deal.

Similarly, when the Supreme Court's 1973 *Roe v. Wade* decision came down, it made abortion a hot and divisive topic nationwide—something it has continued to be to this very day. Throughout the 1970s and into the 1980s, Paul sent mixed messages to his listeners about his position on the issue. But some of his statements clearly seem to indicate sympathy with the abortion-rights cause.

Prior to *Roe*, each state legislature in the nation was slowly working its way through the torturous process of balancing the freedoms of women with the civil and human rights of unborn babies. Different states were finding different solutions based upon the values and will of the citizens of those states. In 1972, New York had some of the most permissive abortion laws in the nation. Texas had some of the most restrictive. Many states were somewhere in between. But in every case, state by state, region by region, the body politic was working its way toward compromise and consensus. This is not unlike what individual states were going through in the 1960s in regard to civil rights. In both cases, the courts terminated this organic process, abruptly pulling the matter out of the hands of the states.

Paul had chastised the courts in the 1960s for this type of activism and circumvention of states' rights on a number of issues. And the same principles made Paul a consistent critic of court-ordered busing right up to and beyond 1973. It is difficult to understand how he could view one as a bad idea and the other as admirable.

Some see a solution to this mystery—Paul's seeming inconsistency with lifelong principles on both the ERA and the abortion issue—in the influence of his bride. Angel had indeed been an ambitious career-oriented woman going back to her graduate student days in St. Louis. And beginning in the 1940s, she had worked in a male-dominated industry. Perhaps her experiences inclined her to encourage her husband to support the ERA. And maybe the fact that Paul had nearly lost his beloved Angel in childbirth made him especially sensitive to the emotional debates over "life of the mother" exceptions built into most proposed abortion laws. Of course, this is all speculation.

Perhaps we must simply write it down to confirmation of George Orwell's observation that we humans have the unique ability to hold two contradictory opinions in one mind simultaneously. If Paul was indeed torn about the issue, it would explain his attraction to an episode of *The Rest of the Story* Paul Jr. would write for him in 1980, a year in which the presence of a strongly pro-life candidate in the presidential race would put the national debate over abortion front and center.

The title of this edition was simply "IF." In it, Paul begins by acknowledging that abortion is a heartrending choice sometimes faced by women whose lives are endangered by pregnancy and by some victims of rape. He then goes on to ask us to put ourselves in the place of a doctor who must advise them:

> . . . *two young women, both pregnant, both doubtful as to*
> *whether they should be. Now, remember: such a choice is*
> *ultimately the mother's, but because you are a physician, and*
> *because your judgment is respected, and because your patient is*

*seeking guidance, everything you say, regardless of how clinically
objective—yes, even the tone of your voice—may sway her
decision.*[14]

One of these women, Caterina, is a poor unmarried teen who
has lost contact with the father of her baby. The other is Klara. She is
twenty-eight and already has three children. All three died of disease
as infants or toddlers. She fears for the health of this baby, too. She
confesses that her husband is actually her uncle, and furthermore,
physical deformities tend to run on her side of the family.

After giving us many sad and disturbing details of these two pregnant women, he asks us how we would counsel them:

So what, Doctor, is your advice?

*In addition to all immediate considerations—physical,
moral, religious—the dilemma of whether to terminate a
pregnancy is a philosophical question:*

*Might this life, if left to live, affect the consciousness or even
the destiny of mankind?*

*Yet if the profundity of this question is diminished by the
balance which governs all life, there is evidence in the two true
stories you have just heard: the unwed mother with unwanted
child; the married mother with the graves of three infants
behind her.*

*For if you, as the hypothetical physician, have opted in both
cases for abortion—then you have respectively denied the world
the multifaceted genius of Leonardo da Vinci—and spared
humanity the terror of Adolf Hitler.*

They are the rest of the story.[15]

Is this broadcast vignette an outward reflection of an inward
struggle by Paul to reconcile the pull of his libertarian instincts with

the directing needle of his moral compass? We don't know. What is sure is that throughout the 1970s, he frequently dismayed his core fans and confounded his critics' attempts to pigeonhole him as a stereotypical conservative.

. . .

The narrow election of Jimmy Carter to the presidency came in 1976. A former California governor had challenged incumbent Gerald Ford in the Republican primary and lost. Ronald Reagan's effort, however, won him many fans across the country, setting the stage for Reagan's successful run against the incumbent Carter four years later. One of those Americans deeply impressed with Ronald Reagan was broadcaster Paul Harvey.

Elsewhere in the world, the last of South Vietnamese resistance collapsed, and Saigon fell to the invading armies of the communist North on April 30, 1975. One of the most famous photos of the twentieth century is the shot of the last U.S. helicopter taking off from the roof of the American embassy there. Beside it are a hundred or more panic-stricken people clambering up a gangway and over each other in hopes of getting on that last chopper. Embassy personnel had to kick at desperate Saigon residents who were clinging to the runners of the aircraft, so it could get airborne.

The day before, a North Vietnamese rocket had hit the Defense Attaché Office at nearby Ton Sun Nhut Air Base, killing two marine security guards assigned to protect it during the evacuation. Corporal Charles McMahon and Lance Corporal Darwin Lee Judge became the last two American soldiers killed in the Vietnam War. This divisive chapter in our nation's history was closed. But the nightmare for the people of South Vietnam, and for millions of others in places like Laos and Cambodia, was only beginning.

The year also brought both frightening and happy news to Paul and Angel concerning their son. Paul Jr. had been pursuing, with some success, a career as a concert pianist, but early in the year he was struck by a car and badly injured. While he was recuperating, he spoke with his father about an idea he'd had for a new radio program. For years, *Paul Harvey News and Comment* had regularly contained interesting, little-known anecdotes about famous people. Invariably at the end, Paul would close the anecdote by saying, ". . . and now you know the REST of the story."

Paul Jr.'s idea was to build a separate, five-minute program around that same concept. His father liked the idea but was already writing two daily newscasts, a television commentary, and three newspaper columns each week. He suggested that Young Paul take a crack at writing the program. Laid up in plaster casts and with nothing else to do, the twenty-eight-year-old did just that.

Young Paul proved to be as gifted a writer as his father. A proud dad often declared his son was actually better. The result was Paul Harvey Jr. becoming the lone writer for the next thirty-two years of one of the most successful radio enterprises of all time—Paul Harvey's *The Rest of the Story.* He found more than a new career in 1976. On October 23, he was wed to Tanya Hastings in a small family ceremony. Classical pianist Van Cliburn was in attendance.

• • •

As most of those who lived through them will agree, the years of the Carter presidency were tough in many ways. At home, there was an energy crisis, rampant inflation, impossibly high interest rates, and unemployment. Internationally, the Soviet Union was on the move all over the world and seemed to be intent on carrying out the Leonid Brezhnev doctrine of encircling and isolating the United States in a global ring of communist client states.

By the end of the decade, the Soviets had invaded Afghanistan and had existing or emerging client states in strategically vital southern Africa and on our doorstep in Central America. The Carter administration allowed America's former ally Iran to fall to Muslim revolutionaries who were now holding Americans hostage. As month after month dragged on, the mightiest nation on earth seemed impotent to do anything about it.

In July 1979, Jimmy Carter gave his now famous "malaise" speech, in which he tried to address the anxieties and frustrations of the American people. In it, he painted a dark picture of the national mood:

> I want to talk to you right now about a fundamental threat to American democracy.
>
> I do not mean our political and civil liberties. They will endure. And I do not refer to the outward strength of America, a nation that is at peace tonight everywhere in the world, with unmatched economic power and military might.
>
> The threat is nearly invisible in ordinary ways. It is a crisis of confidence. It is a crisis that strikes at the very heart and soul and spirit of our national will. We can see this crisis in the growing doubt about the meaning of our own lives and in the loss of a unity of purpose for our nation.
>
> The erosion of our confidence in the future is threatening to destroy the social and the political fabric of America.[16]

President Carter may have been accurate in his grim diagnosis, but this wasn't the brand of leadership that a floundering nation was looking for. Americans didn't want a dire diagnosis; they wanted robust, muscular confidence in sincerely held principles. They wanted a visionary, not a bureaucrat. And Providence was about to give them one.

As for Paul, the eternal optimist did his part to help us keep it all in perspective. When the *Chicago Tribune* asked a number of prominent individuals for some hopeful words amid the gloom, he happily obliged, writing:

> Historians live longer than most. They know that despite the best we can do, recessions come every seven years; that despite the worst we can do, excesses inevitably correct themselves.
> Each generation imagines that we're all going to hell.
> Each generation goes through a little hell and comes out heat tempered and better than before.[17]

As it turned out, Paul wasn't the only one determined to sell the country on itself. The nation was on the edge of emerging from a dark night of self-doubt. It was about to be morning in America.

CHAPTER 11

MORNING IN AMERICA

"Every pessimist who ever lived has been buried in an unmarked grave. Tomorrow has always been better than today, and it always will be."

PAUL HARVEY

THERE'S A DEPRESSION ON. JOBS ARE SCARCE. But he's tall, handsome, confident, and fresh out of college, where he played football. And he's determined to get a job in radio. His heart's desire is to be a sports announcer, but he'll take any radio job he's offered to get a foot in the door.

He started his dream quest by aiming a little too high. He knocked on the doors of the big Chicago radio stations he'd listened to as a kid—WENR, WBBM, and WMAQ—but they told him that, without experience, they couldn't hire him. They suggested he'd be better off trying for a job somewhere "out in the sticks." So he went home to Dixon, Illinois, crossed the river over into Iowa, and found his way to station WOC in Davenport.

He takes the elevator to the top floor, and soon he's shaking hands with a gruff Scotsman who walks with the assistance of two wooden canes. He's looking for an opportunity to prove himself and will do any job, he tells the program director.

"Where were you yesterday, lad?" the older man demands. "We had an announcer position open . . . held auditions yesterday. The job's filled. Where were ye then?"

Shattered, the young man turns and heads back down the hallway toward the elevator. To himself, he mutters, "How the heck can a guy get to be a sports announcer if he can't even get a job at a radio station?" Just as he is reaching for the elevator button, he hears the clack of wooden canes on hardwood floor.

"Hold on a wee second there, you big lug," he says. "Did you say something about *sports* announcing?" he asks.

"Yes, sir, I want to get started in radio because I hope to be a sports announcer eventually."

"Do ye know anything about football?"

"Well, I played football for four years in high school and all through college."

"Could ye tell me about a football game and make me see it as if I was home listening to the radio?"

"Yes, sir, I'm sure I could," the young man replies, hoping what he is saying is true.

He is led into a studio and positioned in front of a microphone. "When the red light goes on," the program director tells him, "start describing an imaginary football game to me and make me see it. I'll be in the next room listening."

A moment later, the red light glows. Twenty-two-year-old Ronald Reagan stares at the microphone for a few seconds and then improvises:

> *Here we are in the fourth quarter with Western State University leading Eureka College six to nothing. Long blue shadows are settling over the field and a chill wind is blowing in through the end of the stadium. . . .*[1]

It is 1933. A few weeks later and six hundred miles away, another small-town boy with big radio dreams will get his start when a supportive teacher escorts him down to the studios of a Tulsa station.

Fifty years later, one of these young men will be the most influential man in America. And the other . . . will be the president of the United States.

As Ronald Reagan takes the oath of office in January 1981, Paul Harvey is one busy man. At an age at which most folks are contemplating retirement, the sixty-two-year-old is still doing two editions of *Paul Harvey News and Comment* each weekday and another on Saturday. *The Rest of the Story*, written by Paul Jr., is wildly popular and airs six times each week. Three times a week Paul writes a syndicated column that is routinely carried by three hundred newspapers. He tapes a daily five-minute TV segment, *Paul Harvey Comments*, that is seen in 120 markets.

Each day, he is heard on 1,075 stations and draws more than 21 million listeners. In a few months, when the spring network radio ratings come out, the results will not be surprising. Four of the ten highest-rated network programs in the nation are Paul Harvey properties—coming in at numbers 1, 2, 3, and 9.[2]

And in his spare time? Well, at $20,000 per speech, he commands one of the highest speaking fees in America, and organizations everywhere are waiting in line to pay it. So two or three times each week he jumps in his private Learjet right after taping his television commentary around 1:00 p.m. and shoots off to some corner of the country to give a dinner speech. He's usually back in his own bed before midnight. Then up at 3:00 a.m. to start again.

His contracts with ABC routinely guarantee him ten weeks of vacation each year. He has rarely taken more than two.

All of this makes Paul one of the most important opinion shapers in the nation. And the peak of his influence has just intersected with the ascendance of a president who is a man after his own heart. And wouldn't you know that president would be a radio man. In fact, Ronald Reagan will soon revive a form of FDR's Fireside Chats, with a weekly Saturday radio broadcast—a practice subsequent Oval Office holders will continue.

Paul's radio career has spanned eight previous presidential administrations. And he has gently, good-naturedly chided each one of them for enthusiastically expanding the size and reach of government, for raising taxes, and for tempting Americans to trade their freedoms for a false security.

Decades earlier, Paul wrote a prayer. It was a plea that God would raise up a certain kind of president for our country. In 1952, he wrote:

> Almighty God, send us a leader.
> A man with his feet planted firmly in American tradition.
> A tall man . . . with his head above the fog of selfish interests.
> Not a common man. This time, God, send us "an uncommon man" . . . a statesman.
> We don't deserve him, but send him anyway.
> And hurry, please. The hour is late. The candle of freedom burns low.[3]

Almost thirty years would pass before Paul would see an answer to that prayer. But in Ronald Reagan, he found a kindred spirit. Over the next eight years, Paul would respectfully disagree with his president on a few key issues. But their commonalities ran wide and deep. Both drew the clear water of their convictions from the same philosophical well. Both drank deeply.

For one thing, the men shared an unshakable belief in what some call "American exceptionalism." It is a belief that there is something unique and wonderful about this nation, and that God ordained both her birth and her rise to preeminence. Ronald Reagan spoke of an

America that was "a land of hope, a light unto nations, a shining city on a hill." And it wasn't just campaign rhetoric. Read his personal diaries and letters and you discover a man who believed those words were true.

Paul viewed America as a miracle of history as well—impossible to replicate or, if lost, impossible to restore:

> I know well from what has gone before, if all this [nation] stands for dies, it will not rise again. Daniel Webster said, "that which has happened but once in six thousand years cannot be expected to happen twice."
>
> This magnificent accident, government under God, will not happen twice. . . .
>
> And one day the trumpet is going to blow, and we shall shout Hallelujah! . . . which way to Paradise?
>
> And the soft, calm voice of Final Authority will say, "You have had it, mister; you have had it."[4]

Somewhere along the way, postmodern educations, creeping agnosticism, and what Reagan famously labeled a "blame America first" mentality had robbed many Americans of any belief that their country was special or even particularly good. In the decades since Reagan left office, that faith has fallen even farther out of fashion.

Today most of the bully pulpits belong to the multiculturalism-obsessed sophisticates who view belief in American exceptionalism as quaint or racist or arrogant or even dangerous. But in 1981 the two most prominent pulpits in the nation belonged to men who preached "America the beautiful" and that God had indeed shed his grace on her in a unique way.

Reagan and Harvey were also profoundly optimistic by nature. This doesn't necessarily come through in their speeches warning about the threat of creeping socialism or the dangers of neglecting our military preparedness. But the fact is, both men held the dual convictions of the inevitability of (capital *P*) Progress and the inherent goodness of the American people.

At the age of eighty, Paul told an interviewer:

> Each morning, I get up like a prospector going panning for gold. I can't wait to get on to the Teletypes and telephones and the copier and find out what foolish and heroic things 200 million people have been doing all night for me to talk about. And each day there's some wonderful, dramatic new breakthrough that opens a whole new horizon of opportunity for us—commercially, socially, culturally. My goodness.[5]

On countless occasions, in speeches, interviews, and casual conversation, Paul repeated these words, "Tomorrow has always been better than today. And it always will be." He believed it, too.

At that point in a Paul Harvey sermonette, Ronald Reagan would have surely said, "Amen." After Reagan's passing in 2004, *New York Times* columnist David Brooks wrote, "Of all the words written upon the death of Ronald Reagan, none have recurred more frequently than 'optimist.' Reagan had a sunny, hopeful disposition, we've been reminded again and again."[6]

Brooks went on to point out how this brand of conservatism differed somewhat from mainstream conservative tradition:

> Conservatives felt that events were moving in the wrong direction and that the American spiritual catastrophe was growing ever worse. Whittaker Chambers observed that when he left communism and joined the democratic camp, he was joining the losing side of history. In his influential book "Ideas Have Consequences," Richard Weaver argued that American society was in the midst of "a fearful descent."[7]

William F. Buckley famously described his conservatism as simply a desperate effort to "stand athwart history, yelling, 'Stop!'"

But to listen to Reagan and Harvey is to hear men who recognize fallen man's tendency to wickedness, and yet clearly believe that the hand of Providence on this nation will pull it upward and forward in spite of itself. Haltingly, perhaps. With seasons of decline and detour. But inexorably upward.

Of Reagan, Brooks said, "He seemed to regard freedom's triumph as a historical inevitability. He couldn't look at mainstream American culture as anything other than the delightful emanation of this venture. He could never feel alienated from middle American life, or see it succumbing to a spiritual catastrophe."[8]

One element of both men's optimism was their absolute delight in technological breakthroughs and scientific advancement. That enthusiasm is in part why Paul was a charter board member of the John D. and Catherine T. MacArthur Foundation—one of the richest private foundations in America and the source of MacArthur "genius grants."

On what would turn out to be the final broadcast of his life—the Saturday *News and Comment* for February 7, 2009—he reported:

> *On the medical front . . . Gene therapy may have cured*
> *eight of ten children with "bubble boy" disease. The* New
> England Journal of Medicine *reports that they are no longer*
> *on medication . . . show no signs of any other problems.*

The legendary voice was thinner and raspier than the one we all remember. The diction, a little less crisp. The modulated highs and lows of inflection, a little less melodic. He was ninety, after all. But his excitement at the prospect of yet another breakthrough on the disease-fighting front was just as tangible. The newsman who had heralded the breakthrough allowing the mass production of penicillin in the 1940s, Jonas Salk's conquest of polio in the 1950s, and the first heart transplant in the 1960s still gushed with genuine wonder at the news of every new advance.

At the crowded intersection of economics and governance, both Paul Harvey and Ronald Reagan viewed progressive taxation as counterproductive to maintaining a strong economy and a properly limited scope of government. But more than that, they viewed it as *immoral*. It offended a deeply held ethic about rewarding work, discouraging sloth—yes, Paul frequently used that King James word *sloth* in his commentaries—and not coveting that which belonged to your neighbor.

In their view, the goal of good government was equality of opportunity, not uniformity of outcome. That meant embracing the hard truth that if one man worked harder and smarter than his neighbor, the laws woven into the fabric of the universe by its Creator would likely reward that man with greater abundance. The right to work and then enjoy the fruit of your labors was a holy thing. As early as 1952, Paul had written:

> This nation was not carved out of the wilderness, as some say.
>
> It was scratched and chopped and dug and plowed and hammered and clawed out.
>
> No government in history ever *gave* its citizens what hardworking Americans with their sleeves rolled up have *earned* for themselves.[9]

In the view of both men, not only was use of a tax code as an instrument for the redistribution of wealth immoral, it was a poor way to raise money for the things government genuinely ought to be doing. High marginal income tax rates discouraged enterprise just as high capital gains taxes discouraged saving and investment—both of which stymied business growth and job creation. This meant lowered revenues to the federal government. "Men don't do big things for small reward," Paul once observed.

It was President Reagan who introduced us all to the Laffer Curve. Arthur Laffer was the economic adviser to President Reagan who pointed out there was a steep diminishing returns curve, followed by a steep negative returns curve, where tax rates and government revenues are concerned. But thirty years earlier Paul had put forth the same logic in his book *Remember These Things*:

> Many years ago it was stated it would appear that success is to be punished; that exorbitant taxes have made it a crime for a man to prosper. The end result of such an order can only be the removal of incentive, the discouragement of our people, and the destruction of our free society.[10]

He was loosely quoting a Greek adviser to the king of Persia from 400 BC.

Given all of the above, cutting taxes was high on Ronald Reagan's agenda. And in the first full fiscal year of his first term, he won approval in Congress for major cuts in the top marginal income tax rates. Of course, an economy the size of the United States's is a big ship to turn. And the passage of that tax cut coincided with the country slipping into a recession.

But the goal of cutting tax rates was twofold. First, it began to address the ethical/moral issue of unfairly punishing success and innovation. But it was also designed to reduce the size of government by starving it. That second goal was more difficult to achieve, however, because the Democrats held firm control of both houses of Congress. Thus, continued high domestic spending combined with the high cost of Reagan's restoration of the country's diminished military capabilities resulted in soaring budget deficits.

Throughout the recession months of 1982 and early 1983, Paul exhorted Americans to be patient and to give the tax cuts time to have their effect. In this season, Paul coined the term *Reaganomics* to describe this seemingly novel approach of leaving more money in the pockets of the people who earned it so they can either save it (providing capital for business investment) or spend it (spurring economic growth).

In 1984 when Reagan was running for reelection against Walter Mondale, a writer for *National Review* described Paul's public cheerleading for Reagan's economic programs this way:

> As recovery indicators grow more numerous, so do Mr. Harvey's exclamation points. "President Reagan has performed a major miracle . . . Our economy is sunnyside-up without inflation! . . . Reaganomics is working!" Nay-sayers and would be bud-nippers are paddled publicly instead of privately in woodsheds: "The recovery is picking up steam. Only Fritz Mondale hasn't heard yet. . . . Domenici has capitulated to Democrats on his Budget Committee. . . . [Media pundits] are visibly dismayed that Reaganomics is working."[11]

Yes, a recovery was well under way in 1984, and what followed turned out to be the leading edge of one of the longest peacetime stretches of economic expansion and job creation in our nation's history.

Clearly, Paul Harvey and Ronald Reagan saw eye to eye on the large majority of issues. But there were exceptions. The most conspicuous of these in Reagan's first term was the issue of U.S. intervention on behalf of anticommunist governments and insurgencies in Central America. Here, Paul's isolationist impulse brought him to a different conclusion than Reagan's "city on a hill" idealism.

It was Reagan's policy to try to shore up an anticommunist government in El Salvador that was fighting a Marxist insurgency and help an anticommunist insurgency trying to displace a pro-Soviet government in Nicaragua. There were a lot of unsavory characters on every side of these conflicts and very few "Boy Scouts." Reagan's logic was: better to have pro-American unsavory characters running the countries in our backyard than pro-Soviet ones. President Reagan also had the force of nothing less than the nearly two hundred-year-old Monroe Doctrine behind him.

But Paul Harvey didn't like it. As Joseph DiSanto later describes in his article "A Lover's Quarrel with Ronald Reagan (Paul Harvey on Foreign Policy in Central America)" in the *National Review*:

> On show after show Mr. Harvey shakes his head over our involvement in Central America. From the conservative newsman's lips come familiar liberal catchphrases. We're getting sucked in by "that same domino theory that motivated our dead-end involvement in Vietnam." Domino theorists are nervous Nellies who fear that if El Salvador goes Communist, eventually "the Reds will be at the Rio Grande."
>
> U.S. intervention, he tells listeners, is unjustifiable because of the "unworthiness of our allies"; it is unsupported by the American people, most of whom "don't even know which side we're on down there"; it is almost certain to fail and perhaps make Ronald Reagan "the first President ever to fall from a slip on a banana republic"; and if it does succeed, it will merely result in the "perpetuation of a ruthless military dictatorship."[12]

In other words, Reagan's belief in American exceptionalism compelled him to favor action in Central America, while Paul's same belief led him to oppose it. So, fifteen years after dismaying many conservatives with his call to withdraw from Vietnam, he did so once more with his opposition to these efforts to keep the Soviets from gaining a foothold on America's doorstep.

Indeed, to the casual listener, a great deal of what Paul Harvey was saying was indistinguishable from the views of vocal celebrities like Ed Asner and Danny Glover. But as DiSanto points out, though he came to a similar position, his reasons were completely different:

> Sounds left-wing, but the sentiments behind the words are rooted in the opposite side of the spectrum. Paul Harvey is an isolationist of the pre-World War II school. New-breed, left-wing isolationists believe the U.S. contaminates countries it tries to help militarily; Harvey believes those countries contaminate the United States. The left-isolationists pronounce America a "sick society" too morally feeble to venture abroad; Harvey finds America so uniquely vital and virtuous that she ought not risk infection from chronically unstable, violent regimes.[13]

Their disagreement on this issue in no way tarnished the admiration and affection Reagan and Harvey felt for one another. In fact, in September 1988, President Reagan and the First Lady served as honorary hosts of a dinner honoring Paul at the Museum of Broadcast Communications in Chicago. The speakers that night included Billy Graham and Larry King.

As for Paul—the man who had entreated heaven for a tall, uncommon, statesman-leader all those years ago—it was especially gratifying to have seen the answer to his prayer in the gift of Ronald Reagan to our nation. How grateful? Consider this: Paul told Larry King in 1988, Ronald Reagan's final year in office: "I'm with Walter Lippmann in thinking a newsman ought to always keep just a little bit of space between himself and the newsmakers. I can't be on a first-name basis with these folks on the Hill and handle the news objectively. That's why through eight administrations I've never had a picture of a president in my office . . . until now."[14]

CHAPTER 12

FINISHING STRONG

"I would love to retire. I would love to change the pace and have more family time, if I could just find something I would rather do. I can't find it. I am so disciplined to sit at this typewriter and paint pictures all morning, I can't find anything more fun."

PAUL HARVEY

Paul Harvey News and Comment
12:00 p.m., September 11, 2001

By now you know . . . just before nine this morning New York time . . . a plane crashed into the side of the World Trade Center . . . exploding on impact. Minutes later another plane crashed into the second tower and exploded. Subsequently, both towers collapsed.

We were next to hear from the Pentagon. That it . . . had been hit.

Suddenly, we were in an undeclared war . . . with enemies . . . that are already dead. Speculation is inevitable. It's hard to guard against an enemy whose religion teaches him that to die for his convictions is a shortcut to heaven. No presently known connection, but at the top of the list of avowed world terrorists, of course . . . is Osama bin Laden.

> *Stay tuned to this station, please, for constant updates on this historic day . . . when our nation . . . when our beautiful nation . . . came of age.*
>
> *Paul Harvey . . . Good day.*

On only one other occasion had that signature sign-off seemed less chipper . . . more world-weary. It was that "Good night" in November 1963 when, after recapping the events of JFK's assassination, Paul closed by predicting that if the end of civilization should come, it would not be bombs or missiles that brought it, but rather the hatred and fear of fanatics.

Now, in the light of September 11's events, that prediction seemed uncannily prophetic. For almost ten years, those with eyes to see could follow radical Islam's slow-motion declaration of war against the West and Western culture's relentlessly encroaching modernity. One of the initial warning shots had been the first World Trade Center bombing in 1993.

Though deeply grieved by the event, in the months that followed 9/11 Paul was cheered by America's response. He had always claimed that patriotism was not dead in America, that it was very much alive in the heartland and simply lying dormant elsewhere. The sudden (and brief) surge of flag flying in bastions of progressivism like San Francisco and Boston immediately after the attacks seemed to validate his belief. He was also heartened by the Bush administration's muscular military response to the attacks, as well as the surge in armed forces enlistments among young people.

In 2003, two years to the week after the event, he tried to help a group of college students put it all in perspective:

> Some of us have been professional observers of several lifetimes. We remember epidemic TB, and the crash of '29, and the dust bowl and Hitler's holocaust and Pearl Harbor. We resent

challenges, but we're no longer panicked by them. Osama bin
Laden epitomizes for this generation what we called hippies or
flower children in the last generation. These anti-establishment
unwashed, counter-culture rich kids have hijacked Islam for
their personal aggrandizement, where the previous generation
of student radicals identified with peace, the seminarian Taliban
spoiled brats espouse holy war, a parallel perversion of a worthy
purpose.

What will it take to get terror and terrorism off Page One?
We already have. Osama bin Laden has much more to worry
about than you do. . . . Bin Laden's press agents had told him
that he had two billion loyal disciples all over the world. They
had him convinced that if he could just knock the top off New
York City, two billion people would rise up all over the world
and on 40 different fronts overthrow us overnight. Not one
did. . . .

Times don't change. Time goes in circles. The atom bomb
altered the potential strategy of war, but we are never without
war for very long. In the 3½ thousand years of recorded history,
fewer than 8 percent of those years have been warless ones.
It's been barely . . . my goodness, it's been barely 138 years
since we were at war with ourselves. So [testing] times are part
of the planet's normal climate. An eternity is being prepared
somewhere, a perfect place, and we have to demonstrate here
whether we deserve to be there. And if there were perpetual
sunshine there would be no victory. So it's testing time again.
From everything I have seen, man alive, we're passing this test
again and with our colors flying.[1]

Paul Harvey. Eternal optimist. Advocate of unsung heroes. Singer
of the praises of small-town champions. Head cheerleader for the
self-reliant and self-sacrificing. This is what he was in the turbulent

opening years of the long-awaited new millennium. And it is precisely what he had been in the decade and a half since his friend and hero Ronald Reagan had left office.

Paul clearly admired our forty-first president, George H. W. Bush. He had been disappointed when Bush caved to pressure from a Democratic Congress and signed a huge tax increase into law—reneging on his dramatic "Read my lips" promise delivered in his nomination acceptance speech at the Republican Convention of 1988—and Paul said so. But he was a strong vocal supporter of the president's assembly of an America-led coalition for the liberation of Kuwait after the Iraqi invasion of 1990.

As should be clear by now, Paul Harvey was far from the knee-jerk warmonger many critics on the Left tried to paint him as after his passing. But Operation Desert Storm was Paul's kind of military operation: American soldiers serving under an *American* flag, a massive overwhelming force designed to make quick work of enemy defenses and minimize American casualties. And Norman Schwarzkopf was his kind of commander: no half measures, no pussyfooting around, no reluctance to use overwhelming American airpower to spare the lives of American soldiers, no hand-wringing about image and public relations. Just get in, get the dirty job done, and go home.

In other words, in Paul's view, Desert Storm had all the elements that were lacking in America's efforts in Korea and Vietnam.

In December of 1991, Paul signed a new ten-year deal with ABC Radio that reportedly paid the broadcaster in the neighborhood of $7 million per year. Even though the man was in many ways a living anachronism—a throwback to the days of John Cameron Swayze and Arthur Godfrey somehow teleported into an age of twenty-four-hour cable news—his listenership had never been higher. In his fifty-eighth year on radio, he was reaching about 23 million listeners each week. This was in large part due to the rise of the popularity of AM talk radio in the late 1980s.

In the 1970s and early 1980s, AM had seemed to rapidly be going the way of the dinosaurs. More and more listeners were migrating to FM for music. And as most of ABC's FM properties switched to rock, pop, or R & B music, Paul's newscasts had increasingly seemed as out of place on these stations as a pair of wing tips on a surf bum. Station after station dropped Harvey's weekday offerings in large markets. Sometimes a smaller, lower-rated station in the market picked them up. Sometimes not.

Then AM stations discovered the conservative talk format. And the format discovered Rush Limbaugh. The rest is radio history.

By 2009, conservative talk radio expositors such as Limbaugh, Sean Hannity, Glenn Beck, Laura Ingraham, Neal Boortz, Dr. Laura Schlessinger, and crossover talents like William Bennett and Michael Medved were drawing huge audiences and had utterly revived AM radio. That revival gave Paul's programs new life and a friendly audience.

• • •

As we have seen, Ronald Reagan was Paul Harvey's ideal president incarnate. Bill Clinton was—to be diplomatic—less so. The reasons revolve just as much around style and character as public-policy differences.

As we've observed, Paul had a highly developed sense of morality. From the very beginning of his career as a commentator, he had shaken his head at off-color humor on the radio and championed a high standard of decency.

In June 1952, he was invited to testify before a House committee investigating declining decency in the young medium of television. Yes, as hard as it may seem given what is currently acceptable fare on network television, there were those who found some of the crude jokes proliferating on television in the early 1950s troubling. As a report in *Time* magazine that year tells us, Paul "insisted he was no prude but that things are so bad he has had to turn off one program (unnamed) 'rather than blush in front of my own wife.'"[2]

As late as 2003, Paul asked, "Isn't there something absurdly incongruous about a society which regulates so rigidly what we put into our mouths and into our nose and so timidly what goes into our eyes and into our ears?"[3]

Paul was an unapologetically old-fashioned advocate of what used to be called clean living. Like a kindly Sunday school teacher, he once told a group of young people:

> And, you know, we can live even longer if we would behave ourselves, if we just practice self-discipline, because most of what ails us is self-inflicted, resulting from smoking and misuse of drugs and venereal disease and overdrinking, overeating. With nothing more than self-discipline, the *New England Journal* is convinced this generation could expect to enjoy an average active hundred years.[4]

Paul personally didn't smoke, and he loathed the tobacco addiction's hold on others. He didn't swear—"my goodness" or "goodness gracious" being the most colorful phraseology you were likely to hear from him. Nor did he drink—except for an occasional glass of wine with dinner. He was so clean, he squeaked. Thus it shouldn't come as a shock to learn that America's philandering, cigar-smoking, former Vietnam War–protesting forty-second president wasn't exactly Paul's cup of tea. In a quip that is as close to being bawdy as we would ever hear the broadcaster make, he once noted that "Mr. Clinton might very likely have his likeness one day engraved on the side of Mount Rushmore, if only from the waist down."[5]

He criticized the awkward "don't ask, don't tell" compromise policy regarding gays in the military and the steep cuts in military spending claimed in the name of a "peace dividend" justified by the collapse of the Soviet Union. He saw both of these as demoralizing to men and women in uniform and damaging to the security of U.S. citizens.

After fifty years of decrying the growth of government, he viewed Hillary Clinton's health-care proposals as some of the most troubling he'd seen out of Washington since the New Deal. But those same principles had him applauding Bill Clinton's courageous welfare reforms that the president got passed despite the objections of most of his own party, and in 1994, Paul broke ranks with most conservatives by expressing reservations about the Whitewater hearings.

• • •

In the early months of 2001, Paul found himself struggling physically with his voice for the first time in his long career. When the problems first developed, he took several days off here and there in hopes of giving his voice some rest and recovery time, but his vocal issues only seemed to grow worse. One morning in May he woke up, tried to speak, and couldn't. His voice was gone.

Months passed, and it didn't return. Even more troubling, the doctors he saw didn't know what to make of it. Paul began to confront the possibility that he might never speak again. He surely felt much like a concert pianist suddenly losing the use of his hands.

In a 2003 interview with Larry King, the host asked Paul what is was like "to not have that voice." The reply, "How can I find the words to answer that question? Since I was fourteen, that voice has been my vocation, my avocation. It's been my life."[6]

The broadcaster went on to elaborate:

> I spent a great deal of time feeling sorry for myself, and then
> settled down at the insistence of my wife and son to start
> making some notes for a book that I had postponed writing.

First, I read . . . twenty-five and a third books. That third [of a book], by the way, was on broadcasting. I couldn't finish that book because it was so full of all those words that I consider inappropriate and offensive. So I spent my time as fruitfully as I possibly could.

After much prayer and more severe testing of Paul's legendary optimism, he and Angel were directed to a respected Chicago ortholaryngologist—one who looked after many of the opera stars of Chicago's Lyric Opera. He identified Paul's problem immediately. A viral infection had attacked one of the broadcaster's vocal cords and weakened it to the point of near paralysis.

A forty-five-minute outpatient procedure implanted a small piece of plastic alongside the vocal cord, reinforcing the muscle until the virus could be eliminated and its strength restored. His voice returned almost instantly. How grateful was the artist to have his instrument back? "I spent a lot of time on my knees that night," he told Larry King.

The restoration of that voice gave us seven more years of the gift that was Paul Harvey. In 2005, he received a special gift from President George W. Bush in the form of the Presidential Medal of Freedom. At the time Paul said, "This is the highest honor I have received since sixty-some years ago, when Angel said 'I do.'"[7]

Through the balance of the Bush presidency, he responded to unfolding news events in ways that were utterly consistent with the convictions and values that he had been bringing to the news since the late 1940s. He had always recognized that war is an ugly, bloody business done by mostly honorable but fallible men making split-second decisions in hellish circumstances. Thus, he defended the ongoing war in Afghanistan and enraged the antiwar Left when he suggested the media was making too big an issue of civilian casualties in a place where the lines between civilians and combatants is so blurry as to be nonexistent. It was the same impulse that led him to give the soldiers working at Abu Ghraib in Iraq the benefit of the doubt. "A pulled-punches war is outrageously expensive," Paul emphasized in one broadcast. He ran afoul of the Council on American-Islamic Relations on more than one occasion—usually for daring to state the obvious.

Nevertheless, throughout the 1990s and right up through Paul's final broadcast, political comment remained only a small part of each program. Each was filled with what he cherished most: stories of unsung heroes, well-told accounts of common people doing stupendously amazing things. Or sometimes amazingly stupid things.

Often the story was told in typically minimalist fashion, allowing the listener to connect the dots. One Chicago radio pro said the consummate Paul Harvey news story was this:

John Smith of Cincinnati, Ohio, decided to have a cigarette before bed last night. . . . He was 62.

Paul never let the news stay too heavy for too long. Each segment of each program contained humor, often of the dry variety:

- *Nudists in Lakeland, Florida, are upset that outsiders are sneaking a peek through a hole in their fence. The police promise to look into it.*
- *A man called the IRS and asked if birth control pills could be deducted. The IRS worker, not missing a beat, came back and said, "Only if they don't work."*
- *White House occupants come and go. They are just like diapers. They should be changed often, and for the same reasons.*

Another feature America came to count on was his celebration of astonishingly long wedding anniversaries. In a tribute after the broadcaster's death, *Kansas City Star* television critic Aaron Barnhart called Harvey "the nation's cheerleader for marriage longevity." He tells this illuminating story about a trip he and his wife made to her uncle Everett's fiftieth wedding anniversary:

> He was the last of a line of seven brothers and sisters born to a southeastern Minnesota farm family, all of whom were fortunate enough to mark their golden anniversaries. At one point during the celebration, the church basement fell silent, and someone played a tape. It was a 30-second clip from a recent Paul Harvey news and comment.
>
> [S]omeone had sent [Paul] a clipping noting the remarkable milestone of the seven siblings. One day, he had decided to share the news with an audience of millions, in that familiar warm, reverent voice. It was way beyond cool. A local achievement had just been celebrated by Paul Harvey. If it had appeared on the front page of the *New York Times*, it wouldn't have been half as impressive to those gathered in that room.[8]

Eventually, after decades of celebrating couples who had been married for six or more decades, Paul and Angel became one of them. In fact, in June 2007, they celebrated their sixty-seventh wedding anniversary. It seemed to many that, like the never-ending *Paul Harvey News and Comment* program, the two would surely just keep on being a couple perpetually.

After sixty-seven years, they still held hands constantly, whether walking out of the studio after a day's work or sitting together watching their nightly one-hour ration of television. In a 2002 interview Angel said, "I love him. I think he's handsome. I love his voice." She sounded like a teenager with her first crush.

He said, "She's a dainty thing. Isn't she lovely? But she has a will of iron."

Of course, nothing this side of heaven lasts forever. Around the time of that anniversary celebration, Paul and Angel had received bad news about her health. "Leukemia," the doctors said. Before the next anniversary could be marked, she was gone. The season Paul would call "the loneliest days of his loneliest winter" had come.

After Angel's passing, he stayed away from work for weeks. Some wondered if the remarkable six-decade run of *Paul Harvey News and Comment* had finally ended. The two had been together almost incessantly since Young Paul had left the nest forty years earlier. Without her, Paul Sr. seemed lost and floundering.

At the urging of his son and dearest friends, Paul did return to the air after a few months of quiet grief. His return was fueled in part by thousands of letters and e-mails he received in that season—messages of deep condolence and profound appreciation. Many of these also carried a pointed question. "We miss you. When are you coming back to us?"

On his first day back, his program began this way:

First, about my own recent absence from this microphone. . . .
A torrent of e-mail to Paul Harvey . . . for which I will be
forever in your debt . . . a torrent of mail to PaulHarvey.com,
is explaining that I owe you for two lifetimes of sharing part of
your days, and then suddenly dropping out of hearing.

Well, I do intend to repay that debt. So gradually these visits
will resume. They will never be the same . . . the loneliest days
of my loneliest winter are still very much with me . . . nothing
I would ever ask you to share, and yet you did.

Paul Harvey News will not be the same as when he had
Angel's twenty-four-hour perspective. I will do my best with
what remains. But it will be something less.

Several months later he stepped away from the microphone again. This time the absence was permanent.

"STRICTLY PERSONAL"

"Ralph Waldo Emerson said it: 'Everyone is criticizing and belittling the times; yet I think our times, like all times, are very good times if only we knew what to do with them.'"

PAUL HARVEY
Autumn of Liberty

THE TITLE OF THIS CONCLUSION IS BORROWED from Paul Harvey. The man whose fingers tapped out roughly 40,000 newscasts and 3,600 newspaper columns wrote only two full-sized books—both of them in the 1950s. *Remember These Things* (1952) and *Autumn of Liberty* (1954) are filled with powerful and important arguments about serious subjects like war, taxes, liberty, Marxism, treason, and the relentless march of history. But both books close with a chapter called "Strictly Personal." In each instance, Paul sets aside politics and policy and weighty world affairs. Instead he gives us startling access to his poet's soul and moving glimpses into his most treasured hours.

As it turns out, the newsman who spent sixty years typing out ten- and twenty-second headlines and stringing them together into fifteen-minute units is a gifted essayist. It is not the familiar Paul Harvey of corny "bumper snickers" and "Page Two" sales pitches for Bose radios we find on these pages. It is an extraordinarily talented writer—one we find ourselves wishing we'd discovered sooner and are saddened that he didn't find time to write this way more often.

Here we find beautiful ramblings about his farm, his dog, the unexpected sunburn that leads to the revelation that he's losing his hair, priceless moments with his son as a toddler and, of course, his Angel.

For example, there is a great little passage in *Remember These Things* about Reveille. The toy cocker spaniel puppy had been a homecoming gift from Angel to Paul upon his return from the army in 1944. Until "Small Paul" came along five years later, Rev was their only "child." Later, when they bought the three-hundred-acre farm on the bluff of the Mississippi, they named it after the dog—Reveille Ranch.

In the middle of a long essay about the family pet, we read:

> Reveille had never been told she was a dog and probably wouldn't have believed it, anyway. She was a little girl, very much a member of the family, and owned twenty-five per cent of its voting stock.
>
> Her bed was the foot of my own.
>
> Perhaps at this point I should explain that I am the man you so often see on the city street . . . two hundred plus pounds and six feet two and with the tiniest dog in the block at my side. My feeling for Reveille is just a mite absurd by the standards of sensible folks; I would not pretend otherwise.[1]

And then a little further on:

> We didn't let ourselves think little Reveille's story would ever have to end . . . until last December. This, they said, was not an illness all man's skill could match.
>
> Angel and I hoped and worked and hid the hurt to salvage small Paul's Christmas . . . and hers.

Before I finish, let me say . . . whenever the pets of others have passed away and my broadcast has been moved to mention them, friends . . . warm, generous, sympathetic . . . have offered the disappointed one another pet to replace the loss.

Please, in this case, try to understand and respect this sincere wish. I will not have another. I don't mean this to sound blunt or ungrateful.

One day, some older, small Paul will have his. But I have had my dog. Her name was Reveille.[2]

On thinning hair . . .

A man who once laughed at ladies for trying to fight time with cosmetics cannot very well complain aloud now in his own behalf.

I have timed this thing so badly . . . so very, very badly. Television on the way in at the same time my hair is on the way out.[3]

Of course he eventually solved this problem with a toupee. He never tried to hide the fact that he wore one. He would openly talk about having to go put on his "TV hair" before taping a program.

On fishing . . .

Every man remembers one love affair, one fight, and one fishing hole.

But his memory emphasizes what he expected of each . . . and forgets what really happened. That the big one . . . got away.

Recent years I've been week-ending in the roadless Canadian forest north of Minnesota.

Endless lakes lined with a sky-high tapestry of trees.

The unmolested Quetico-Superior country . . . land of bear, moose, and occasional visiting elk. And no parking problems.

The tall and uncut land of ten million telephone poles . . . and no telephones.

There, a few hours from my desk . . . wilderness.

It's great therapy . . . matching wits with the whole outdoors by day . . . letting it sing you to sleep at night.

A man may not live any longer . . . but he lives wider . . . and deeper.[4]

On being a dad . . .

And then one day my son was five years old.

That morning, behind one of Chicago's great expressionless stone faces overlooking Lake Michigan, a very big little boy of four approaching the breakfast table turned the corner.

It was fifty-eight minutes past six, and suddenly he was five.

So began for him a happy day of presents, party cake, and play, but Mommy and Daddy find themselves, at once, pulling and pushing. Helping with one hand, holding with the other, as a small boy throws himself against the tender mesh of their affections . . . so restless to rush ahead . . . so impatient to be a man.

My son is five. So *boy*, he sometimes irritates . . . so *baby*, he forgives our irritation . . . milk teeth to molars . . . bittersweet.

Henceforth he ever may play at pretending but . . . never can he really be Superman again. My son is five.[5]

Later in the same piece, Paul gives voice to that mysterious mix of pride and pain every parent feels in watching a child head off to school for the first time. He poignantly expresses the sense of loss fathers and mothers experience as they see the mile markers on a child's road to adulthood flying by too quickly. Referencing Korea's bloody "Heartbreak Ridge," Paul foreshadows the reluctance he'll one day feel when his son reaches the age of military service in a time of war:

The torrent sweeps on. Youth, white water dashing over the sharp edges of broken toys . . . down toward where the current slows before it goes to sea.

I deeper sigh to see this uncomplicated time slip by . . . this magic time of four and before . . . this infant while when, washing himself, he'd always get marooned on one spot or another.

The monkey-like mixed-up happy talk.

Soon school . . . beginning of the effort that it costs to be a man. Cruel eviction from the temperate climate of his treasure island. Teddily, the bear, and Dee Dee, the rag dog . . . orphaned.

Please none with indifference profane this sacred hour when parents hurt. For wherever, anywhere, we walk beside them . . . even as another mother walked with her Son to the crest of the hill to the foot of the Cross . . . so parents yet, in helpless silence, walk beside their sons to sudden manhood on the brow of Heartbreak Ridge.

It is such a little while since that other Sunday . . . five years ago. Oh, God of little boys, be near beside . . . unveil tomorrow with Thy gentlest touch for those two bright eyes, sparkling with the reflection of five candles.[6]

And then there was Angel. As noted in a previous chapter, a good friend of the Harveys considered their relationship "the greatest love story" he'd ever witnessed. In *Remember These Things*, we find Paul offering some thoughts about his bride as their anniversary approaches.

> If it's true, and I think it is, that a man does not start living 'till he's married . . . I'll be twelve soon.
>
> There'll be a dozen roses for my Valentine this year.
>
> Some sensible gift—warm if wearable, nourishing if edible; if valuable, negotiable. She'll understand. And a dozen roses.
>
> The day is still a week away, but years timed with a stopwatch have taught me to be everywhere and do everything early. So, as I say, she'll understand.
>
> What does a man remember most about twelve years, when they're gone and the mystery is spent? When he knows what glamour looks like on the ironing board, what does a man remember? Polynesian moonlight through a Venetian blind . . . and cabbage soup.[7]

As the tender tribute continues, we find more affectionate teasing about Angel's early-married cooking skills. We also hear a clear reference to those first career stops in Missoula, Kalamazoo, and Tulsa as he describes their domestic joint venture as a "happy partnership":

> I remember her a gentle warrior. Tears over trifles, and yet such courage in crises as would have awed King Arthur.
>
> A Phi Beta Kappa key, carefully worn where it wouldn't show. And, in the beginning, soup. Sometimes three days straight.
>
> The beauty of the Bitterroot Valley, Michigan snow, and the Oklahoma Tire and Supply Company at Sixth and Boston. Hard work, in a world so small we had to squeeze into it.
>
> Happy partnership, each too busy rowing to rock the boat.[8]

He recalls some of the treasured mementos of the first twelve years of a lifelong romance, with a special nod to those months of separation during Paul's stint in the service:

This I remember. In memory's black satin casket, these are my jewels.

A book of Browning, bound in hand-tooled leather.

The rose bowl that cost my lunch allowance for a month.

A snapshot of her in a sweat-soaked wallet from the left breast pocket of an army shirt.

Homecoming.[9]

As the anniversary essay winds to a close, Paul entrusts to our view the contents of the deepest recesses of his heart. He reveals those things that this man in midlife most cherishes—a farm, the birth of an adored son that has almost cost him more than he could bear, and a future empty nest with the love of a lifetime:

Together we built ourselves a farm. Felt proud a mile deep. Transplanted two family trees. Carpeted a hillside and a house. The house part, hers. Civilized with tile in the bathroom, porcelain in the kitchen . . . and mousetraps in the basement.

We would retire, I said, while we were young. And we will, for indeed we still are. This thinning hair does not mean what you think. I'll lose it early. Everything early. She'll understand.

. . . And then one day a dream. The valley of the shadow. A miracle. A son. Soft, strong chains.

And yet, he hurries so past youth. Already eager to be somewhere early. So like his dad; she'll understand.

And one day the robin will flutter from the nest, and she'll be mostly mine again.

A dozen roses.

Perhaps this year I'll write a sentimental note. I've not made poems for such a long time now. It won't have to be very good, but she'll like it. It won't make sense to others, but she'll keep it.

Call it a premium on my best investment.

For of stocks and bonds and real estate and bank accounts . . . she, alone, is all that I can take with me when I die.

Though, God willing, I'll go first.

I don't want to be late. And I wouldn't want to wait . . . alone. She'll understand.[10]

In the end it was the other way around, of course. She went first. But only by a little. You have to love that part about "retiring early," though. Goodness, he lived to be ninety and was on the air a week before he passed away!

He missed her desperately, of course. And we will miss him. After his father's passing, Paul Jr. said, "My father and mother created from thin air what one day became radio and television news. So in the past year, an industry has lost its godparents and today millions have lost a friend." And at his father's memorial service, Young Paul repurposed the words his father had read after the death of FDR: "A great tree has fallen and left an empty space against the sky."

One longtime friend quipped, "Paul Harvey's views were like skinny neckties. They never changed. They would just come in and go out of style."

At this writing, it seems the man's views have never been more out of fashion. The size, reach, and power of government are expanding at a breathtaking pace, and a large percentage of Americans seem to view this as a good thing. The loudest voices in the public square are of those demanding a government solution to every ill, an ironclad federal guarantee against every risk, and a regulatory regime for every aspect of American life. Paul's view that people who succeed should be applauded and emulated rather than vilified and punished seems quaint in a season in which members of Congress fan the fires of class resentment with reckless rhetoric. His ideal of an America in which "citizens stood on their own feet and asked nothing for nothing and elected leaders to match"[7] has never seemed so remote and implausible. And yet . . .

If he were still with us, one suspects he would not be wallowing in despair. Delivering stern warnings? Oh, yes. Gently but pointedly upbraiding the big spenders and high taxers? No doubt. Praising the courageous politicians who throw themselves in front of a panic-driven regulatory juggernaut? Absolutely.

But he wouldn't be declaring that all is lost or that America is doomed or that her greatest days are behind her. You see, he had been here before. He knew that years don't necessarily add wisdom, but, my, they do add perspective.

He had been among those who thought the sky was falling in the forties with FDR's New Deal. He had been deeply concerned about encroaching socialism in the fifties; shaken his head at the sexual and cultural revolution of the sixties; been made to feel like a "displaced person in his own country" in the seventies; yet witnessed the birth of renewal in the eighties; and seen a surge of reawakened patriotism after 9/11.

He would be concerned about our nation. But he would also pass along Miss Harp's advice to a frightened, angry little Tulsa boy: "Just do all that you can as long as you live to preserve this last wonderful land . . . in which any man willing to stay on his toes . . . can reach for the stars."

And he would also be quick to remind us: "Tomorrow has always been better than today. And it always will be."

That's just the way things work in Paul Harvey's America. . . .

Good day.

PAUL HARVEY
MAXIMS

People don't dare big things for small rewards.

Love what you do, or do something else.

Never feel resentment for those who have more than you. Remember we live in a wonderful land in which any man willing to stay on his toes can reach for the stars.

You can't make a small man tall by cutting the legs off a giant. Punishing success never advances the lot of the struggling in the long run.

You never accomplish anything by talking over the heads of others.

As long as you are imitating someone else, the most that you can ever hope to be is second best.

A faith you only borrow from your parents cannot endure. Ultimately you have to own it for yourself.

It is important to build an intellectual base for your goals. Formal education is fine. Self-education is vital.

The virtues of hard work, self-reliance, and personal initiative make America a land of opportunity in which anyone willing to work a little harder than the next guy and go the extra mile can succeed.

The basic American creed of the founders and pioneers was: I believe in my God, my country, and myself. And in that order.

There is no easy success. No free lunch. No guaranteed rocking chair.

Wars should be fought only if necessary and only to win—with our best weapons and our best tactics.

The greatest threat to America is not an attack from outside— but rather a slow internal surrender by her people to the illusory seduction of the welfare state.

The temptation to swap liberty for false comfort of government-guaranteed security is a fool's bargain.

Storms are a part of the normal climate of life.

Tomorrow is always better than today. It always will be.

It is a foolish and self-destructive society that punishes success and makes it a crime for a person to prosper.

Reporters can't be on a first-name basis with politicians and handle the news objectively.

We can live longer if we behave ourselves—if we just practice self-discipline. Most of what ails us is self-inflicted.

All of our times are good times, if only we know what to do with them.

THE QUOTABLE
PAUL HARVEY

"When I was a boy I fell in love with words . . . ran away and joined the radio."

"My job is to make what is important, interesting. And what is interesting, important."

"I am fiercely loyal to those willing to put their money where my mouth is."

"If life were logical it is men who would ride sidesaddle."

"Just by turning to the Left . . . the world has gone in circles."

"I'm just a professional parade watcher who can't wait to get up every morning and get to the curbside."

"In times like these, it helps to recall that there have always been times like these."

"I've never seen a monument erected to a pessimist."

"Like what you do; if you don't like it, do something else."

About Ronald Reagan:
"I'm with Walter Lippman in thinking a newsman ought to always keep just a little bit of space between himself and the newsmakers. I can't be on a first-name basis with these folks on the Hill and handle

the news objectively. That's why through eight administrations I've never had a picture of a president in my office . . . until now."

"I am a salesman. And until the day they nail the lid on that box, I will be. And until that day, my primary focus will be keeping our God-blessed United States of America . . . sold . . . on itself."

"The economic vehicle we rode to the top is free competitive American capitalism! Do not let the word 'Capitalism' frighten you. It has been abused, misused, and maligned and slurred like some naughty word nice people do not use . . . but capitalism has been our good servant. Yet some want to trade a good servant for a bad master."

"Trust me to paint pictures on the mirror of your mind and I will let you feel such agony and ecstasy, such misery and majesty . . . as you would never be able to feel by merely looking at it."

"The years don't always add wisdom, but they do add perspective."

"I am satisfied with all my heart that if Uncle Sam ever does get whipped, it will have been an inside job. It was internal decay, not external attack, that destroyed the Roman Empire."

"We wanted security. And they gave us chains. And we were 'secure.'"

"Americans, there's an election going on all the time. The Lord votes for you, the devil votes against you, and you cast the deciding vote."

"Let us with the conscience of reasonable men preserve and protect and defend this last great green and precious place on earth against all its enemies . . . foreign and domestic, so help us God . . . if only because so many people you never knew have broken their hearts to get it . . . and to keep it for you."

"Each generation imagines that we're all going to hell. Each generation goes through a little hell and comes out heat tempered and better than before."

"*I know well from what has gone before, if all this [nation] stands for dies, it will not rise again. Daniel Webster said, 'That which has happened but once in six thousand years cannot be expected to happen twice.' This magnificent accident, government under God, will not happen twice.*"

PAUL HARVEY
AWARDS AND HONORS

2005—Presidential Medal of Freedom awarded by President George W. Bush

2003—*Radio&Records* News/ Talk Lifetime Achievement Award

2002—Received the Marconi Award for the fifth time

2000—Tex McCrary Award for Journalism from the Congressional Medal of Honor Society

1999—*Broadcasting & Cable* magazine included Paul Harvey as one of "The Men of the Century"

1998—The Marconi Award, Network Personality of the Year

1998—*George* magazine included Paul Harvey as one of "The Twentieth Century's Most Significant Americans"

1998—Gold Angel Lifetime Achievement Award

1997—Radio Mercury Lifetime Achievement Award

1996—The Marconi Award, Network Personality of the Year

1996—American Spirit Award, United States Air Force

1995—*Broadcasting & Cable* magazine Hall of Fame Award

1994—American Advertising Federation Silver Award

1994—NAB Spirit of Broadcasting Award

1994—The Peabody Award

1992—Toastmasters International Outstanding Public Speaker Award

1992—Good Guy Award, American Legion

1991—Paul White Award, Radio Television News Directors

1991—The Marconi Award, Network Personality of the Year

1991—Interstate's Great American Race Legends Award

1991—The Board of Directors Award, National Religious Broadcasters

1990—William Booth Award, Salvation Army

1990—Emerson Radio Hall of Fame Award

1990—Dante Award

1990—Chicago Hall of Fame Journalism Award

1989—The Marconi Award, Network Personality of the Year

1989—International Radio Festival Journalism Award

1989—"Others" Award, Salvation Army

1989—Gold Medal Award, International Radio & Television Society

1989—Lowell Thomas Award

1987—James Herriot Award, Humane Society of the United States

1987—Henry G. Bennett Distinguished Service Award, Oklahoma State University

1986—Genesis Award, The Fund for Animals

1985—Certificate of Appreciation, Humane Society of the United States

1984—Certificate of Meritorious Service Award, American Academy of Family Physicians

1984—Outstanding Broadcast Personality, Advertising Club of Baltimore

1983—Horatio Alger Award

1982—Best Speaking Voice Award, American Speech, Language, Hearing Association

1982—Golden Radio Award, National Radio Broadcasters Association

1981—Man of the Year, Broadcast Advertising Club of Chicago

1980—General Omar N. Bradley Spirit of Independence Trophy

1980—Outstanding Broadcast Journalism, Boston University

1980—Father of the Year, Father's Day Council

1979—National Association of Broadcasters Hall of Fame

1975—John Peter Zenger Freedom Award

1975—American of the Year, Lions International

1955—Oklahoma Hall of Fame

SUGGESTED READING

Remember These Things by Paul Harvey (The Heritage Foundation, 1953)

Autumn of Liberty by Paul Harvey (Hanover House, 1954)

Our Lives, Our Fortunes, Our Sacred Honor by Paul Harvey (W Publishing Group, 1985)

Destiny: From Paul Harvey's The Rest of the Story by Paul Aurandt (Paul Harvey Jr.) (Bantam, 1984)

Paul Harvey's The Rest of the Story (Doubleday, 1977)

More of Paul Harvey's The Rest of the Story edited by Paul Harvey Jr. (William Morrow, 1980)

Paul Harvey's For What It's Worth by Paul Harvey Jr. (Bantam, 1992)

The Selected Letters of William Allen White 1899–1943 edited by Walter Johnson (Henry Holt and Co., 1947)

Home Town News: William Allen White and the Emporia Gazette by Sally Foreman Griffith (Oxford University Press, 1989)

NOTES

Introduction

1. Katy Bachman, "Harvey Hangs Ten: ABC Radio Re-Signs 82-Year-Old Broadcaster to New Contract," *Mediaweek*, November 6, 2000, http://www.allbusiness.com/services/business-services-miscellaneous-business/4808777-1.html.

2. Nellie Andreeva, "Harvey Stays Tuned to ABC," *Hollywood Reporter*, November 2, 2000, http://www.allbusiness.com/services/motion-pictures/4824214-1.html.

3. Rick Kogan, "Good Days for Paul Harvey," *Chicago Tribune*, August 4, 2002, http://www.chicagotribune.com/entertainment/chi-paul-harvey-good-days-rick-kogan,0,6707009.story?page=2.

4. Ibid.

5. Ibid.

6. Phil Rosenthal, "Paul Harvey: An Appraisal of His Career by the Tribune's Phil Rosenthal," *Chicago Tribune*, March 2, 2009, http://www.chicagotribune.com/news/columnists/chi-harvey_rosenthalmar02,0,6976104.story.

Chapter 1: A Stubborn Reverence

1. Ron Owens, *Oklahoma Heroes: A Tribute to Fallen Law Enforcement Officers* (Paducah, KY: Turner Publishing Company, 2000), 41–42.

2. Paul Harvey, "Address at Police Week 1992," National Law Enforcement Officers Memorial Fund Banquet.

3. Paul Harvey, "What Are Policemen Made Of?" Law Enforcement Articles, http://www.lawenforcementarticles.com/what-are-policemen-made-of.

4. Montgomery College History Department, "The Tulsa Race Riot of 1921," Montgomery College, http://www.montgomerycollege.edu/Departments/hpolscrv/VdeLaOliva.html.

5. Stephen Kerr, "Tulsa like You've Never Heard It Before," *Perspectives*, May/June 2003, http://www.pcusa.org/oga/perspectives/mayjune03/tulsa.htm.

6. Ibid. A Scottish composer, Lindsay Davidson, has written a three-act opera featuring orchestral bagpipes in honor of Dr. Charles W. Kerr and his efforts to avert a human tragedy.

7. Marc Fisher, "Still Going," *American Journalism Review*, http://www.ajr.org/Article.asp?id=2348.

8. Paul Harvey, "Homecoming" (Tulsa, Oklahoma, April 2, 1994), quoted in Philip M. Crane, *Congressional Record* 140 (August 5, 1994): E1664, http://thomas.loc.gov/cgi-bin/query/z?r103:E05AU4-206.

9. Paul Harvey, *Autumn of Liberty* (Garden City, NY: Hanover House, 1954), 42.

10. Ibid., 43.

11. Ibid.

Chapter 2: The Voice of Oklahoma

1. Philip Crane, *Congressional Record* 140 (August 5, 1994).

2. Interview with Paul Harvey, "A Chat with Paul Harvey," *Programmer's Digest*, December 31, 1973.

3. Rick Kogan, "Good Days for Paul Harvey," *Chicago Tribune*, August 4, 2002.

4. Paul Harvey interview by Larry King, *Larry King Live*, CNN, 1988.

5. Ibid.

6. As quoted in Mike Thomas, "Paul Harvey," *Salon*, September 25, 2001, http://dir.salon.com/story/people/bc/2001/09/25/harvey/print.html.

7. Paul Harvey, *Remember These Things* (Chicago: The Heritage Foundation, 1952), 10–11.

8. Harvey interview, "A Chat with Paul Harvey," *Programmer's Digest*.

9. Paul Harvey, "The Landon Lecture," Kansas State University, Manhattan, KS, September 19, 2003, http://www.k-state.edu/media/newsreleases/landonlect/harveytext903.html.

10. Paul Harvey, "I Found My Quiet Heart," *Guideposts*, June 1972, http://www.dailyguideposts.com/archive/archive.asp?archID=GPAOE.

Chapter 3: Behind Every Successful Man . . .

1. Paul Harvey interview by Larry King, *Larry King Live*, CNN, 1988, http://www.museum.tv/newssection.php?page=510.
2. Ibid.
3. George M. Watson Jr., *Winged Shield, Winged Sword 1907–1950: A History of the United States Air Force*, ed. Bernard C. Nalty (Honolulu: University Press of the Pacific, 2003): 1:259.
4. Harvey interview, *Larry King Live,* 1988.
5. "The *Real* Paul Harvey: Stand by for News!" *Esquire*, November 7, 1978.

Chapter 4: A Wide-Angle View of America

1. Paul Harvey, "Farewell, Paul Harvey," WGN, Chicago, 2009.
2. Paul Harvey interview by Larry King, *Larry King Live*, CNN, 1988, http://www.museum.tv/newssection.php?page=510.
3. "Beverly Hills Club Will Pay Honor to Home," *Chicago Daily Tribune*, October 12, 1947.
4. Joe Howard, "Harvey: A Legend Looks Back," *Radio Ink*, November 2, 2006, 24.
5. "Paul Harvey to Receive Disabled Veterans' Award," *Chicago Daily Tribune*, October 7, 1945.

Chapter 5: My God, My Country, Myself

1. "WENR-TV Air Debut Tonight to Present an Array of Talent," *Chicago Daily Tribune*, September 17, 1948.
2. Savage, "The Tower Ticker," *Chicago Daily Tribune*, January 19, 1949.
3. Joe Howard, "Paul Harvey: A Legend Looks Back," *Radio Ink*, November 6, 2006, 24.
4. Phil Rosenthal and Gerry Smith, "Paul Harvey Dead at 90," *Chicago Tribune*, February 28, 2009.

5. Rick Kogan, "Good Days for Harvey: Contract Will Keep Radio Newsman Busy," *Chicago Tribune*, August 4, 2002.

6. Associated Press, "Lynne Harvey: Broadcaster's Wife Was Force behind Scenes; Producer Helped Paul Harvey Ensure Listeners Knew 'The Rest of the Story,'" *Chicago Tribune*, May 4, 2008, http://archives.chicagotribune.com/2008/may/04/news/chi-hed_harvey_wife_04may04.

7. "Driver at Work under Auto Dies in Triple Crash," *Chicago Daily Tribune*, August 7, 1950.

Chapter 6: Un-American Activities

1. Willard Edwards, "College Profs Tell Why They Became Reds," *Chicago Daily Tribune*, January 28, 1951.

2. "Paul Harvey Seized Inside Atom Lab Area," *Chicago Daily Tribune*, February 7, 1951.

3. Steve McGregor, "Argonne Passes a Reporter's Security Test," Argonne National Laboratory, February 6, 1996, http://www.anl.gov/Media_Center/News/History/news960206.html.

4. "Harvey's Atom Lab Case to Go to Grand Jury," *Chicago Daily Tribune*, March 17, 1951.

5. "Kerner to Read FBI's Report on Harvey Seizure," *Chicago Daily Tribune*, February 13, 1951.

Chapter 7: Cold War, Hot Emotions

1. Paul Harvey, *Remember These Things* (Chicago: The Heritage Foundation, 1952), 87.

2. Ibid., 89.

3. Ibid., 102.

4. Ibid., 14.

5. Ken Layne, "And Now You Know . . . He's Dead," *Political Machine*, February 28, 2009, http://news.aol.com/political-machine/2009/02/28/and-now-you-know-hes-dead.

6. Richard Corliss, "Paul Harvey: The End of the Story," *Time*, March 1, 2009, http://www.time.com/time/arts/article/0,8599,1882444,00.html.

7. Glenn Garvin, "Fools for Communism: Still Apologists After All These Years," *Reason*, April 2004, http://www.reason.com/news/show/29095.html.

8. Ibid.

9. Linda Witt, "Forget Cronkite: Paul Harvey Is the Biggest Newscaster in America, and Getting Bigger," *People*, January 22, 1979, http://www.people.com/people/archive/article/0,,20072778,00.html.

10. Paul Harvey, *Autumn of Liberty* (Garden City, NY: Hanover House, 1954), 23–24.

11. Harvey, *Remember These Things*, 73.

12. Ibid., 176–177.

Chapter 8: A Snapshot in History

1. Paul Harvey interview, *Programmer's Digest*, vol. 2, December 31, 1973.

2. Paul Harvey, *Autumn of Liberty* (Garden City, NY: Hanover House, 1954), 13–14.

3. WGN audio archives, http://caster.wgnradio.com/Harvey/harveywordpictures.mp3.

4. Quoted in obituary for Milton Friedman in the *Wall Street Journal*, http://www.ssc.wisc.edu/~mchinn/miltonfriedman_WSJ17nov06.pdf.

Chapter 9: The Great Unraveling

1. As recalled by Cal Thomas, "No One Can Replace the Great Paul Harvey," *Fox Forum*, February 28, 2009, http://foxforum.blogs.foxnews.com/2009/02/28/thomas_harvey.

2. John McCain and Mark Salter, *Faith of My Fathers* (New York: HarperCollins, 1999), 186.

3. Phil Rogers, "Paul Harvey Remembered," NBC Chicago, March 2, 2009, http://www.nbcchicago.com/news/local/Paul-Harvey-Remembered.html.

4. Paul Harvey interview by Larry King, "Special Tribute to Paul Harvey," *Larry King Live*, CNN, March 1, 2009, http://transcripts.cnn.com/TRANSCRIPTS/0903/01/lkl.01.html.

Chapter 10: The Decade of Doubt

1. Paul Harvey, "I Found My Quiet Heart," *Guideposts*, June 1972, March 30, 2009, http://www.dailyguideposts.com/archive/archive.asp?archID=GPAOE.
2. Ibid.
3. Ibid.
4. Ibid.
5. Ibid.
6. Paul Harvey interview by Larry King, "Special Tribute to Paul Harvey," *Larry King Live*, CNN, March 1, 2009, http://transcripts.cnn.com/TRANSCRIPTS/0903/01/lkl.01.html.
7. Phil Rogers, "Paul Harvey Remembered," NBC Chicago, March 2, 2009, http://www.nbcchicago.com/news/local/Paul-Harvey-Remembered.html.
8. "The Hero Calley," *Time*, February 15, 1971, http://www.time.com/time/magazine/article/0,9171,904698,00.html.
9. Paul Harvey interview, *Programmer's Digest*, WKDA Nashville, December 31, 1973.
10. Joe Howard, "Harvey: A Legend Looks Back," *Radio Ink*, November 2, 2006, 20.
11. Paul Harvey, *Autumn of Liberty* (Garden City, NY: Hanover House, 1954), 95.
12. Ibid., 88–89.
13. Ibid., 96–97.
14. Paul Harvey Jr., *More of Paul Harvey's The Rest of the Story* (New York: William Morrow & Co., 1981), 11.
15. Ibid.
16. Jimmy Carter, "Crisis of Confidence," televised speech, July 15, 1979, http://www.pbs.org/wgbh/amex/carter/filmmore/ps_crisis.html.
17. Paul Harvey, "Ten Chicagoans Think Positively about the Future," *Chicago Tribune*, January 5, 1975.

Chapter 11: Morning in America

1. Ronald Reagan, *An American Life* (New York: Simon & Schuster, 1990), 65.
2. The weekend editions of *The Rest of the Story* and *Paul Harvey News and Comment* are considered separate programs.

3. Paul Harvey, *Remember These Things* (Chicago: The Heritage Foundation, 1952), 137.

4. Ibid., 71.

5. Noel Holston, "Harvey Still an Optimist after All These Years," *Minneapolis Star Tribune*, November 17, 1998, http://www.highbeam.com.

6. David Brooks, "Reagan's Promised Land," *New York Times*, June 8, 2004, http://www.nytimes.com/2004/06/08/opinion/reagan-s-promised-land.html.

7. Ibid.

8. Ibid.

9. Harvey. *Remember These Things,* 9.

10. Ibid., 64–65.

11. Joseph DiSanto, "A Lover's Quarrel with Ronald Reagan: Paul Harvey on Foreign Policy in Central America," *National Review*, February 24, 1984, http://www.highbeam.com/doc/1G1-3146524.html.

12. Ibid.

13. Ibid.

14. Paul Harvey interview by Larry King, "Special Tribute to Paul Harvey," *Larry King Live*, CNN, March 1, 2009, http://transcripts.cnn.com/TRANSCRIPTS/0903/01/lkl.01.html.

Chapter 12: Finishing Strong

1. Paul Harvey, "Landon Lecture," Manhattan, KS: Kansas State University, September 13, 2003, http://www.k-state.edu/media/newsreleases/landonlect/harveytext903.html.

2. "Where Is the Line?" *Time*, June 16, 1952, http://www.time.com/time/magazine/article/0,9171,859733—00.html.

3. Harvey, "Landon Lecture."

4. Ibid.

5. Ibid.

6. Paul Harvey interview by Larry King, "A Special Tribute to Paul Harvey," *Larry King Live*, CNN, March 1, 2009, http://transcripts.cnn.com/TRANSCRIPTS/0903/01/lkl.01.html.

7. Aaron Katursky, "Paul Harvey's Wife Dies at Age 92," ABCNews.go.com, May 3, 2008.

8. Aaron Barnhart, "Remembering Paul Harvey, the 'Invisibles' Man," *TV Barn*, March 1, 2009, http://blogs.kansascity.com/tvbarn/2009/03/paul-harvey-the.html.

Conclusion: "Strictly Personal"

1. Paul Harvey, *Remember These Things* (Chicago: The Heritage Foundation, 1952), 168.

2. Ibid., 170–171.

3. Ibid., 174.

4. Paul Harvey, *Autumn of Liberty* (Garden City, NY: Hanover House, 1954), 177–178.

5. Ibid., 181–182.

6. Ibid., 182.

7. Harvey, *Remember These Things*, 164.

8. Ibid., 164–165.

9. Ibid., 165.

10. Ibid., 165–167.

ABOUT THE AUTHORS

STEPHEN MANSFIELD is the *New York Times* best-selling author of *The Faith of George W. Bush*, *The Faith of the American Soldier*, *The Faith of Barack Obama*, and *Never Give In: The Extraordinary Character of Winston Churchill*, among other works of history and biography. Founder of both the Mansfield Group, a research and communications firm, and Chartwell Literary Group, which creates and manages literary projects, Stephen is also in wide demand as a lecturer and inspirational speaker. For more information, log on to http://www.mansfieldgroup.com.

DAVID A. HOLLAND is an author, speaker, and media consultant who fell in love with radio as a boy; started working in radio stations in college; and subsequently worked as a news director, on-air personality, and director of affiliate relations for a national news-talk network. He is a founding partner of Cobalt Bridge Multichannel (http://www.cobaltbridgemultichannel.com) and a creator, producer, and syndicator of talk radio programs. David lives in Dallas.